The Politics of Media Scarcity

This book questions the predominance of "media abundance" as a guiding concept for contemporary mediated politics. The authors argue that media abundance is not a universal condition, and that certain individuals, communities, and even nations can more accurately be referred to as media scarce – where access to media technologies and content is limited, highly controlled, or surveilled.

Through case studies that focus on guerilla militants, incarcerated Indigenous people, and cold war-era infrastructure, including Soviet "closed" or "secret" cities and Canadian nuclear bunkers, the book's chapters interrogate how the once media scarce later "speak" to – and can be heard by – the predominant, abundant media culture. Drawing from several art projects and diverse cultural sites, the book highlights how media scarce communities negotiate and otherwise narrate their place in the world, their past experiences and lives, and escape from subjugation. To better understand media scarce politics, the book asks how and when communities become – by accident or force, by choice or necessity – media scarce.

This innovative and insightful text will appeal to students and scholars around the world working in the areas of media and politics, art and politics, visual studies, surveillance studies, and communication studies.

Greg Elmer is Professor and Bell Media Research Chair in the School of Professional Communication at Toronto Metropolitan University, Canada.

Stephen J. Neville is a PhD candidate in the Communication and Culture program at York University and Toronto Metropolitan University, Canada.

Routledge Focus on Media and Cultural Studies

Community Media and Identity in Ireland
Jack Rosenberry

Cultural Chauvinism
Intercultural Communication and the Politics of Superiority
Minabere Ibelema

Crowdfunding and Independence in Film and Music
Blanka Brzozowska and Patryk Galuszka

Building Communities of Trust
Creative Work for Social Change
Ann E. Feldman

Secrecy in Public Relations, Mediation and News Cultures
The Shadow World of the Media Sphere
Anne Cronin

Spanish Horror Film and Television in the 21st Century
Vicente Rodríguez Ortega and Rubén Romero Santos

Gender-Based Violence and Digital Media in South Africa
Millie Phiri

The Politics of Media Scarcity
Greg Elmer and Stephen J. Neville

The Politics of Media Scarcity

Greg Elmer and Stephen J. Neville

LONDON AND NEW YORK

First published 2024
by Routledge
4 Park Square, Milton Park, Abingdon, Oxon OX14 4RN

and by Routledge
605 Third Avenue, New York, NY 10158

Routledge is an imprint of the Taylor & Francis Group, an informa business

© 2024 Greg Elmer and Stephen J. Neville

The right of Greg Elmer and Stephen J. Neville to be identified as authors of this work has been asserted in accordance with sections 77 and 78 of the Copyright, Designs and Patents Act 1988.

All rights reserved. No part of this book may be reprinted or reproduced or utilised in any form or by any electronic, mechanical, or other means, now known or hereafter invented, including photocopying and recording, or in any information storage or retrieval system, without permission in writing from the publishers.

Trademark notice: Product or corporate names may be trademarks or registered trademarks, and are used only for identification and explanation without intent to infringe.

British Library Cataloguing-in-Publication Data
A catalogue record for this book is available from the British Library

Library of Congress Cataloging-in-Publication Data
Names: Elmer, Greg, 1967– author. | Neville, Stephen J., author.
Title: The politics of media scarcity / Greg Elmer, Stephen J. Neville.
Description: London ; New York : Routledge, 2024. | Series: Routledge focus on media and cultural studies | Includes bibliographical references and index.
Identifiers: LCCN 2023052084 (print) | LCCN 2023052085 (ebook) | ISBN 9781032504681 (hardback) | ISBN 9781032504698 (paperback) | ISBN 9781003398639 (ebook)
Subjects: LCSH: Mass media—Political aspects. | Information behavior. | Mass media—Social aspects. | Information technology—Social aspects.
Classification: LCC P95.8 E46 2024 (print) | LCC P95.8 (ebook) | DDC 302.23—dc23/eng/20231108
LC record available at https://lccn.loc.gov/2023052084
LC ebook record available at https://lccn.loc.gov/2023052085

ISBN: 978-1-032-50468-1 (hbk)
ISBN: 978-1-032-50469-8 (pbk)
ISBN: 978-1-003-39863-9 (ebk)

DOI: 10.4324/9781003398639

Typeset in Times New Roman
by codeMantra

This book was largely written during a very difficult period in all of our lives. The COVID global pandemic affected everyone in some way, whether they contracted the virus, were hospitalized, or tragically lost a loved one. We are unspeakably grateful for the selfless service of all the healthcare professionals that saw us through this terrible collective crisis and continue to face burn out and other challenges due to the pandemic's long aftermath. Thank you for your sacrifices. As a consequence, we dedicate this book to nurses, doctors, and other healthcare professionals.

Contents

	Acknowledgements	ix
1	Introduction: the limits of abundant media	1
2	Media scarcity in apartheid South Africa	14
3	Retracking incarceration: Cheryl L'Hirondelle's ceremonial infrastructure	29
4	Re-staging the Soviet secret city: the good life, the toxic life	44
5	Bunker media: messages from the abundant and redundant underground	60
6	Conclusion: future politics of media scarcity	81
	Index	*91*

Acknowledgements

This book would not have been possible without the ongoing conversations with – and constructive feedback from – Lucas Freeman, Nick Taylor, Jeremy Packer, Ahn Phan Vu, Chris Russil, Isabel Löfgren, Julia Velkova, David Cecchetto, Casey Robertson, Henry Warwick, and Ganaele Langlois.

Our acquisition and managing editors at Routledge, Suzanne Richardson and Stuti Goel, were supportive and encouraging from the very outset and throughout the writing process. Two anonymous reviewers also provided excellent guidance for our early revisions. Thanks also to Erika Biddle for producing the book index.

Early versions of chapters were presented at the Canadian Communication Association's annual conference, the *Vertical Media* conference at York University, the Film and Media speakers series at the Toronto International Film Festival Lightbox, and during Greg's visiting fellowship at Södertörn University in Stockholm. Feedback at these events was crucial in redeveloping and expanding our disparate studies into a cohesive manuscript. We would particularly like to thank Anne Kaun, Fredrik Stiernstedt, Rianka Singh, and Carolyn Kane for providing such engaging venues to discuss our work.

An early version of Chapter 2, "Media Scarcity in Apartheid South Africa", first appeared in the journal *Media Culture and Society*. We thank the journal for permission to republish a greatly expanded and revised version here. Our understanding of African National Congress (ANC) politics developed through numerous discussions with former operatives and cadres. Greg would also like to thank Teddy Mattera, Ethel Williams-Abrahamse, Christopher Webb, and Tristan Vogt for their helpful input. The inspiration for the chapter came from discussions with organizers and film-makers at the *Encounters* Documentary film festival in Johannesburg and Cape Town where Greg screened his feature film *The Canadian Delegation*.

We would like to thank Cheryl L'Hirondelle for her incredible work and generous correspondence, Kinanâskomitin. We are honoured to have been given the opportunity to write about *Why the Caged Bird Sings* and its offshoot projects. We also would like to thank L'Hirondelle's many co-writers for crafting such powerful songs: Margaret Sewap, Tracey Gamble, Shelene

Holcomb, Michelle Marsh, Karen Moocheweines, Angela Rabbitskin, Lisa Smith, Carla Johnson-Powell, Charli Thingelstad, Danielle Ermine, Doris Banahene, Jane Paul, Jeannine George, Stacy Gunnlaugson, Maureen Montgrand, Elizabeth "Lizzie" Charles, Bernice Bighead, Deanna Renee, Desjarlais, Melody Bird, M. Henderson, Jennifer Houle, Rosanna N., Celeste Whitehawk, Abby Nawakayas, Cheyanne Fox, Jessie LaPlante Sandi, Catherine McAlinden, Christine Griffiths, Heike Irmgard Hagen, Sherry Wright, Beverly Fullerton, RM Gorman, Lori ann Maurice, Kristen Dillon, Katie Brunet, Tiffany Peters, E. Jackman, Panda Bear Delorme, Vonetta Martin, Cyndi Sinclair, Bannock Kid, Cruz, Ryder, IWA, AWCP, Lil Durk, Redman, Lil Bear, Key Lo G, Biter, E. Carrier, Kendall Whitstone, Jessica Smith, Faron Longman, Alexis Arcand, Janelle Umpherville, Janelle Montgrand, Carla Johnson, Trevor Alexander, Trevor S. Ballantyne, John Craig, Jayden Laprise, George Lathlin, Donovan Misponas, Fabian Shalthanee, Jake Toutsaint, Robert Young, Alfred Sanderson, Drew Ballantyne, Mitchelle Ballantyne, Larry Bird, Cory Halkett, Joshua Johnson, Randall Lemaigre, Keith William Martell, Robert pachapis Favel, Alfred Sanderson, Gregory Hoskins, Mark Schmidt, Joseph Naytowhow, and Glenn Ens. Maarsii.

Chapter 3 includes three photographs provided courtesy of Cheryl: L'Hirondelle.

Figure 3.1 is a still from one of ten videos from artwork/installation titled *Here I Am* (2013), originally commissioned by curator Steve Loft for exhibition titled *Ghost Dance: Activism. Resistance. Art* at Ryerson Image Centre, Toronto, ON. Videos were created during *Reconsidering Reconciliation* thematic art residency at Thomson Rivers University (Ashok Mathur) and financially supported by The Shingwauk Archive, Algoma University (Jonathan Dewar), and Dylan Robinson (Canada Research Chair, Queen's University). *Here I Am* is part of the permanent collection of the Indigenous Art Centre, Gatineau, QC ,videography by Gabriel Archie; artistic direction by Cheryl L'Hirondelle.

Figure 3.2 is an exhibition still of *Here I Am* (2013) artwork/installation from *Standing Up, Sitting In and Sounding Out* exhibition, Art & Media Lab, Isabel Bader Centre for the Performing Arts, Queen's University, Kingston, ON, October 18, 2016. Carina Magazzeni and Ellyn Walker, curators. Photo by Liz Cooper Photography.

Figure 3.3 is an exhibition still of *Here I Am* (2013) from *Why the Caged Bird Sings: Immersive Engagements* exhibition, The Mann Gallery, Prince Albert, SK. Curated by Judy McNaughton for Common Weal Community Arts. Photo by Tia Furstenberg.

Our secret cities chapter would not have seen the light of day without the photography of Gregor Sailer and Sergey Novikov's insightful, brave, and collaborative art. We can't wait to see their next projects! The chapter was first published as a short commentary in the *Canadian Journal of Communication*. We thank the journal for granting permission to publish a substantially revised and expanded version here. Research for the *Bunker Media* chapter benefitted from the decades-long archival work of Dave Peters and Connie Higginson-Murray. An earlier version of the chapter appeared in the journal *Culture, Theory and Critique*. We thank the editors for permission to republish a revised version here.

The key concepts in the book were first envisioned while Greg and Steve were both supported by visiting fellowships at Erasmus University. A big thanks again to our hosts Jason Pridmore, Dan Trottier, Amanda Alencar, Rashid Gabdulhakov, Anouk Mols, and Qian Huang. Steve would like to recognize funding from the MITACS Globalink programme for the stay in Rotterdam. Funding for the book as a whole came from an insight research grant from the Social Science and Humanities Research Council of Canada and the Bell Media Research Chair at Toronto Metropolitan University.

During the pandemic, Steve overcame a medical emergency due to an incredible team of physicians, nurse practitioners, registered nurses, and many others. In particular, he would like to thank Dr. Khalaf, Dr. Lepic, Dr. Rosart, Dr. Matino, Dr. Iorio, Dr. Al-Housni, Dr. Bali, NP Leach, NP Kolm, RN Kay, other physicians, and countless other nurses and hospital staff who have given him a new lease on life. Steve would also like to honour the contribution of his partner, Amanda Tully-Luong, whose loving caregiving has been constant and is cherished.

1 Introduction
The limits of abundant media

The industrial revolution produced its fair share of utopian classics, from *Looking Backward, 2000–1887* (Bellamy 1888) to *Ionia: Land of Wise Men and Fair Women* (Craig 1898). Such fictional stories typically offered fantastic imaginaries of a technologically rich, efficient, and socially ordered future. Even before the invention of the atomic bomb, the effects of mass industrialization also created apocalyptic, existential imaginaries. One such "introverted world" (Wells 1905, 15), where the world's population sought shelter from a post-solar freeze that rendered life on the planet's surface uninhabitable, was penned by French philosopher Gabriel Tarde – an author best known for his theories of social imitation (2013). However, in Tarde's novel *Underground Man* (1905) even the death of the sun cannot destroy an abundant and rich human society, though H.G. Wells's preface believes the story is offered "half mockingly" (1905, 15). Prior to the sun's demise, the novel recounts the excesses of life on earth, the "superficial and frivolous", the "saturated" ears, filled with music and culture, a planet that saw [the] "…waterfalls, the winds and the tides had become the slaves of man" (Tarde 1905, 23, 32, 43). There had even been an abundance of "pretty women and handsome men" (35).

As Tarde's last remaining communities seek shelter amid the warmth of the planet's core, his new civilization still retains if not enhances its abundant riches. Cultural assets are simply moved underground, somehow saved from the ever-advancing ice age. And indeed, the ice is itself transformed into great symbols of cultural abundance – "…we shall transport enormous blocks of [ice]…to supply the public fountains" (80). Thus "after a more or less long period of settling in [underground], civilized life could unfold anew in all its intellectual, artistic, and fashionable splendour" (80). Tarde's underground life is thus imagined as even more abundant than life on the surface – it promises a new subterranean life replete with an "inexhaustible larder", a "vast library containing all the principle works" and "interminable galleries" (81, 88, 96). In short, the new underground civilization would "never suffer from famine, nor from shortness of supplies" (103). Homeless or cramped? Not a problem in the underground, as Tarde's inhabitants create yet more space for themselves and those seeking their own private spaces by simply burrowing

DOI: 10.4324/9781003398639-1

2 Introduction: the limits of abundant media

further downward into the earth. In short, even an apocalyptic event cannot displace Tarde's abundant society.

Over a century later, while environmental threats have exponentially expanded, our culture has arguably been more fixated on – and defined by – an abundance of media. The internet revolution of the early 2000s, intensified by the widespread use of smart mobile phones and social media platforms, has no doubt produced an imaginary of abundance. Or some might say *overabundance*. As the world faces devastating wars, nuclear threats, growing forms of socio-economic disparities, waves of forced migration, dramatic climate changes, and the rise of ultra-nationalist and fascist parties and governments, we have yet to fully appreciate – and moreover fully critique – the limits of this media abundant world and its seemingly endless consumer choices. Nonetheless, this "media-rich" (Daft and Lengel 1986) or saturated environment has become one of the most predominant frameworks for the study of media today.

Empirically, it would be foolhardy to deny or ignore the scale of media growth, in terms of channels, substacks, platforms, apps, news outlets, websites, or other properties that enable the dissemination of news, opinions, entertainment, or seemingly banal reflections on – and glimpses of – everyday life. The evolution and intensification of media rich infrastructure, first through satellite, then fibre optic cable, and more recently wireless infrastructure, has, since roughly 2000, facilitated an explosion in media content and properties. In turn, through a range of communication practices, "self-produced media" (Croteau 2007) has likewise fundamentally changed the media landscape. According to Statista (2022), every minute in 2022 there were 231,400,000 emails sent, 1,700,000 pieces of content published on Facebook, and 5,900,000 searches made on Google. With the rapid development of digital infrastructure and affordable data plans, video streaming is also on the rise, be it free video platforms or subscription services. In 2022 one million hours of content were reportedly streamed by users worldwide per minute.

But the conceptual turn to media abundance of late cannot be fully explained by advances in media, technology, lowered costs, or user adoption. Theories of media abundance have also emerged as a result of a wide array of social, political, and economic challenges such as attention deficit disorder, media addiction, the disruption of media and news business models, and, of course, the inability to determine fact from fiction. Media abundance has become a shorthand explanation of these social ills, a convenient and moreover largely uncontested term used as a common starting point for both digital media critics concerned about democracy and online harms (Andrejevic 2013; Bastani 2019; Keane 2014; Milligan 2013) and polemically populist scholars that highlight its democratic and pluralistic nature (Boczkowski 2021; Bruns 2019).

Pablo Boczkowski's recent award-winning monograph entitled *Abundance: On the Experience of Living in a World of Information Plenty* (2021), for example, argues that even those who are economically poor and precarious – such as homeless youth – are seemingly media abundant through their use of smartphones. While Boczkowski recognizes the "material scarcity" of the homeless, he fails to recognize how *media* might also be scarce (xii). The argument therefore falls into a binary trap, with media critics being accused of negating user agency and the abundant choices provided by the media landscape. Moreover, Boczkowski's "media abundance" downplays the discriminatory power of media or, worse, suggests that the world is so media abundant that media scarcity is just not a problem. Karppinen (2009, 2) articulates this point succinctly, arguing that:

> In contrast to long-standing concerns for homogenisation of content and concentration of media power, many accounts of the contemporary communicative abundance present an image of almost infinite choice and an unparalleled pluralization of voices that have access to the public sphere... With more information available in public than ever before, concerns for media pluralism and diversity appear to have become not only increasingly contested, but for some, analytically obsolete or anachronistic.

While Mark Andrejevic's *Infoglut: How too Much Information Is Changing the Way We Think and Know* (2013) avoids depoliticized conclusions, like many other digital media critics, he also adopts a media abundant framework. Andrejevic argues that the overload or glut of information produced by the abundant media system has produced a corresponding set of managerial regimes and control technologies. Yet without using the exact term, Andrejevic does implicitly argue that media abundance leads to a *scarcity* of democracy, an argument that has gained greater attention with the emergence of algorithms and artificial intelligence systems (Pasquale 2015). And while Andrejevic offers an important corrective to Boczkowski's more dismissive treatment of the media scarce, he too begins and largely restricts his analysis to the hegemony of the media abundant world.

Of course, ideologies of abundance came well before the digital media age: symbols of the abundant life, economy, and future were embraced and celebrated by the nobility and ruling classes in an effort to maintain and extend hegemonic forms of political power. Even if an admission is made that there may not be enough for everyone – for example, employment, housing, energy, educational opportunities, and food and water – the issue is often downplayed or outright dismissed. To maintain power, moments or pockets of scarcity are said to be fleeting or part of the natural order of life, rarely if ever the fault of government, the monarch, or church. The built environment was used to reaffirm the link between abundance and governmental power. Architecturally ornate statues, fountains, and impressive towers memorialize the innate political power and legitimacy of monarchs and military leaders. One such fountain built in 1815 in Madrid, the centre of the colonial Spanish empire, was named "Fuente de la Abundancia" (Fountain of Abundance), a tribute to King Ferdinand VII. The symbolism of constantly flowing water, the source of life that seemingly never ends, is only matched by the repetitive use of female figures and other associated signs of fertility and reproduction (Esetena 2010).

A culture of abundance remains deeply integrated in cultural practices. In China, the celebration of abundance is communicated through the omnipresent symbol of fish or 鱼 or *yú*. The Cornucopia, or 'horn of plenty', has similarly signified an abundant culture through its overflowing fruits and vegetables. Likewise in Japan, fish has been a central staple and symbol used to celebrate the seasons and bountiful crops in much the same way that Americans place a turkey at the centre of the table to, historically at least, give thanks for the bounty of the harvest (Hegeler 1911, 391). Deities and other symbols of infinite and mythical power likewise reproduce such tropes. In Hegeler's study of Japanese symbols of religion, he begins with an image of Benten, the Japanese Goddess of Divine Love, carrying a basket with a fish. While typically associated with Greek mythology and more recently American Thanksgiving, Indian scholars have also noted the dissemination of the horn of plenty throughout the subcontinent (Borumand 2018, 178).

In addition to symbolic and cultural expressions, early Western theories of communication have also been framed as abundant. For example, Erasmus's theory of writing was predicated upon *copia* (Latin for "abundance"), the ability to always have a written contribution to any potential subject matter. As a form of pedagogy and authority then, Erasmus stressed the need to overproduce, to constantly write again and again (Cummings 2014). The abundant writer was the master communicator, always ready to intervene in debate.

Throughout the world then, symbols of abundance have served to communicate economic stability and hence the legitimacy and power of political and religious institutions, ideologies, and leaders. Abundance has been domesticated through images of sustenance, ritualized through seasonal and religious celebrations, and integrated into the teaching of writing. To question these deeply ingrained forms of cultural and political power, our book adopts a third definition of abundance, the "relative degree of plentifulness" ("Definition of abundance" 2023). We interpret media *abundances* as a matter of degree and political contingency, from the plentiful, overflowing, and even excessive to the point of "decadence" (Keane 2014), on to what we refer to as *media scarcity*, the relative absence of media objects, documents, or archives. Such a definition, and rethinking of the predominant perspectives on media abundance, provides an opening, an opportunity to question when, to whom, and under what conditions media is more or less abundant, focusing in particular on the political complications of *when it is decidedly scarce.*

Our argument also insists that media abundance is not a constant or universal condition. Rather many individuals and communities around the world – as we detail in our book's chapters – experience moments or even prolonged and entrenched cultures of media scarcity. We don't therefore refute the power of abundant media, yet nor do we believe it comforts and provides for all. Rather, we question the social and political demands that media abundance produces, particularly on the media undocumented, those that have lived underground lives, or continue to be media scarce. There is, in short, a politics of media scarcity, a politics at the margins and *below* the media abundant world.

In recognizing and defining media abundance as a form of governmental power, this book offers another mediated landscape, one defined by *scarcity in abundance*. As the world becomes saturated with media content, the more it normalizes, expects and in some cases outright *requires* media documents, archives, pictures, photos (etc.) to confirm and legitimize identities, historical accounts, and political rights. Consequently, personal media archives and objects are essential digital documents required not only to be noticed but also to be *recognized* in the so-called "attention economy" (Williams 2018). Thus, the greater or insistent the requirement for individuals to possess media histories and documents to "participate" in this abundant media environment, the more media scarcity becomes a pressing social and political issue, and a concept in need of recognition, development, and interrogation.

Media scarcity

Media scarcity refers to the lack or loss of media objects and archives challenging how an individual or community narrates, promotes, or otherwise tells stories about their past, present, and future. When we speak of the "undocumented", we must also recognize the role of media, and the mediatized world, the expectations and conventions of abundant media, and the use of media objects and archives as forms of currency, identity, and authority. This point consequently speaks to the central concern of this book – the plight of the media scarce, those who have "gaps" in their mediated histories, or seemingly total absences, be they family photos and albums, diaries, videos, or other media documentation of personal and collective histories. Other media scarce individuals and communities have actively avoided media capture, resulting in limited or no media objects. And then there are still others who assume other identities as a form of political evasion or obfuscation. Such "undercover" individuals may be captured by media, but their true identities remain masked – they also remain media scarce.

Individuals, communities, and even nations can, in some circumstances, be conceptualized as *media scarce* – where access to media content is limited or heavily censored. Authoritarian regimes have increasingly limited access to the internet and some platforms, while also censoring and banning opposition and non-state voices (Billard and Duggal 2022). Yet media scarcity can also impact liberal nations, where under the guise of "security" information and media is severely curtailed. And while this book touches on some of these broader sociopolitical issues, histories, and institutions – namely the impact of geopolitical conflicts, political struggles, colonialism, and incarceration – we are largely concerned with how media scarcity produces various forms of social, political, and economic insecurity in distinct communities and at particular times.

Like theories of media abundance, media scarcity has been amplified by the digitization and datafication of the media industries and indeed across almost every facet of daily life. Manovich's *The Language of New Media* (2002) remains a canonical starting point for both a computational and a broader cultural understanding of the digitization of media. Manovich highlights how discrete media objects, with unique identifiers, locations (URLs), and formats (pdfs, gifs, etc.), are assembled together to tell stories. Associated computer software and programs further amplified the potential of non-linear storytelling, or at least the construction of stories through non-linear means. In such an environment, media objects emerged as digital "assets" or as communicative objects that could be lengthened, brightened, "cleaned", or otherwise changed to better fit the aesthetic or semantic goal of the storyteller.

Media objects have also become central components – the digital assets – in non-linear forms of storytelling and editing. Documentary film has thus greatly benefitted from the process of digitization, where stock footage and other previously hard to acquire image and sounds are now made more accessible through online archives and collaborations with other filmmakers. The "database" documentary has subsequently given new life to the found footage film, where stories are told by drawing upon various sources and digital media objects from around the globe.

The production of – and access to – digital archives has consequently taken on an added importance in the age of digital media objects, in the so-called abundant media environment. While libraries, museums, governments, the courts, and other institutions have struggled to fund, organize, and conceptualize how to digitize and organize their collections, corporate media giants Apple, Facebook (Meta), and others have fully integrated the personal archive into social media accounts, handheld devices, and everyday forms of communication such as email. Each object, be it a photo of a party, a tweet, or an email to a family member, is logged, archived, and made shareable to social networking platform users.

Part of this book's critique of media abundances is, however, not just predicated upon the proliferation of media objects and archives (empirically speaking, through the growth of sources of digital media files, documents, and objects); it also recognizes the infrastructural imperative of media sharing and storytelling, and that platforms and media devices are increasingly designed to encourage media sharing. This is an important point that Jenkins, Ford, and Green (2013, 7) largely gloss over in *Spreadable Media*, a book that seems committed to emphasizing the frictionfree possibilities of the networked era at the expense of those who might have little media objects to share:

> The spreadability paradigm assumes that anything worth hearing will circulate through any and all available channels, potentially moving audiences from peripheral awareness to active engagement.

As media files are digitized and integrated into platforms, media objects-as-documents are imbued with special significance, they are more than "made shareable". The means through which we now read, write, and capture video and sound are increasingly coupled with the process of uploading and otherwise sharing to a variety of online platforms, properties, and communities. While the smartphone's camera app offers the possibility of sharing images to a bevy of platforms, image-focused apps such as Instagram and TikTok are designed to offer users a variety of sharing and recreation options. The expectation or goal of such apps, in other words, is to share media objects. In such media environments, a culture of sharing has emerged, where the user base co-constructs conventions and thus develops expectations of how one shares and what one shares.

As socio-technical documents designed to be shared, media objects have become forms of recognition, identity, and authority. We thus build upon Lisa Gitelman's (2014) conceptualization of documents as both material and ephemeral, particularly in the political sense of the term. She writes: "Documents are integral to the ways people think as well as the social order that they inhabit... [they] can never be disentangled from power – or, more properly, control" (5). Media documents, objects, and platforms therefore do much more than make normative or "conformative" demands of us. They are not simply designed to be shared, rather they also convey power and authority through their use as historical forms of proof and identity. On a personal level, they also function as mandatory political documents, necessary to access adequate housing, education, income, residency, citizenship, and other forms of personal and collective security. Governmental and economic institutions also make demands for personal media objects that, if not met, carry significantly more serious implications than missing a social gathering or having one's haircut commented upon by online friends. For non-residents in Canada, for example, photos are required to establish the authenticity of a marriage as one step toward an approved residency application. The same is true of a plethora of insurance claims, or other mediated forms of "proof", in a range of transactional, legal, juridical, and governmental processes. One's personal history of media, archives, and objects, in other words, are not just shareable reputational capital-objects, they also serve as proof of the right to a range of government and private sector services and programmes. Media objects have, in short, become essential social and political documents.

Becoming media scarce

To better understand media scarce forms of politics, recognition, and storytelling, our book chapters often begin by asking how and when communities become, by accident or force, by choice or necessity, media scarce. We question how communities lose or never produce personal and community media documents, objects (photos, diaries, videos, etc.), and archives, such as individuals who assume other identities or otherwise "go underground". Furthermore, we highlight the pitfalls and challenges of leaving such protected places and personas. Ultimately this takes us to the question of how the once media scarce later "speak" to – and can be heard by – the predominant, abundant media culture. The questions posed in this book highlight how media scarce communities negotiate and otherwise narrate their place in the world and their past experiences and lives, and escape from subjugation. In short, we question how media scarce experiences refashion underground life to confront political and economic injustice and oppression.

It would, however, be a serious mistake to assume that media scarce communities are powerless or voiceless. There are many individuals and communities that proactively choose to avoid the gaze of media, who actively avoid being captured and/or identified by media technologies. Some might claim that such individuals and communities seek privacy from an all-seeing eye. But there is much more here than the need or desire to be left alone or forgotten. Media scarcity, much like privacy, should not be equated simply with anonymity (Kerr, Steeves and Lucock 2009).

Some communities may become media scarce as a result of their wanting to avoid persecution, deportation, discrimination, detention, or worse. In avoiding persecution, the mediation of life can dwindle, stop, or become masked, foreclosing particular life chances and possibilities of social or political recognition. Media scarcity should therefore also be conceptualized and understood as a tactic, as an effort to subvert the mainstream, and to resist, challenge, and disrupt it. Yes, media scarcity is shaped by surveillance, but media scarce individuals and communities can also actively engage and politically challenge the forces of a surveillance-dominated world. The media scarce might engage in practices of "sousveillance" (Mann and Ferenbok 2013) by "watching the watchers", yet this is often paired with other practices that articulate more subtle forms of resistance to power. For instance, the media scarce might engage in acts of "obfuscation" for the goals of "buying some time, providing cover, deniability, evading observation, interfering with profiling, and expressing protest" (Brunton and Nissenbaum 2015, 4). Like obfuscation, media scarce resistance is often enacted through concealment and deception to go undetected or hide in plain sight.

Lastly, media scarce conditions are often born of political histories and struggles, often colonial ones. The likelihood of becoming media scarce or being forced to become so is often a by-product of historical patterns of oppression, and the history and legacy of racism and colonialism. Thus, the marginalizing effects of media scarcity typically perpetuate pre-existing politics and histories of political marginalization, colonialism, precarity, and discrimination. Yet again, we seek to build upon the work of other writers and researchers who have focused on political struggle, on the possibilities of social justice, of empowering those communities challenged by scarcity *in* abundance. Simone Browne's *Dark Matters: On the Surveillance of*

Blackness (2015), for instance, offers a compelling example of the resistance to the history of Black slavery and racism. In an important intervention in studies of surveillance, Browne details how runaway slaves in their pursuit of freedom sought to evade surveillance through a variety of means: using makeup, "wicked tricks", and, for some, hiding in plain sight by passing with false identities (54–55). Indeed, the Underground Railroad brings forth an imaginary infrastructure of Black emancipation, yet we cannot forget about the involvement of false identities, secretive tactics, and cover stories in the individual and collective pathways of escape. As a consequence, we conceptualize the process of actively becoming media scarce as a process of *going underground*. The term is offered to frame the forms of subterfuge and the subterranean politics of identity that intersect with media scarce lives and politics. We deploy both imagined and material definitions of underground life.

More broadly the underground has long been conceived of as a subversive space, a place where counter-cultural norms and conventions are cultivated and honed. Think of underground political or cultural movements or an underground music scene. And while many might seek refuge in underground cultures and spaces, we argue that they do not simply "hide" from the dominant culture and forms of authority. Rather, the underground is a time and space where identities can be forged and rearticulated. The underground is, in this respect, a shelter, but one with its own stories. The underground, in other words, is an active site of identity formation and reformation, away from the glare of media industries and technologies. More broadly, we must not lose sight of the political forms of resistance grounded in conditions of media scarcity from those who are forced to go underground in helping us to imagine a more just and equitable world. In this book, we engage in a worldbuilding politics, a speculative politics of the past, present, and future that, most importantly, does not simply imagine limitless or even greater riches that can be sustained even after an apocalyptic event – as Tarde lays out in *Underground Man*. Rather, we find kinship and inspiration in a range of media scarce politics, past and future stories that emerge out of the underground, as expressed by Ruha Benjamin (2018, n.p.):

> Yes, subordination, subjugation, subaltern, literally "under the earth," racialized populations are buried people. But there is a lot happening underground. Not only coffins, but seeds, roots and rhizomes. And maybe even tunnels and other lines of flight to new worlds, where alternative forms of kinship have room to grow and to nourish other life forms and ways of living.

Organization of the book

Following this introductory chapter, the book is organized around a set of case studies. The examples of former South African militants, incarcerated Indigenous women, residents of "secret" or nuclear cities, and the cold war bunker are not meant to provide a unified theory of media scarcity or to conflate the unique experiences of such disparate communities and spaces. Rather, the diversity of experiences is used to speculate on a range of tactics used by the media scarce to tell their stories to reflect upon their underground experiences, the masking of their identities, and their engagement (or not) with the dominant abundant media culture.

Chapter 2 turns to the decades-long battle against white minority or apartheid rule in South Africa. While much has been written about the African National Congress (ANC) leadership, notably Nelson Mandela's iconic status, and the transition of the party into government in 1991, much less is known about the party's military wing and guerrilla movement that he also founded, uMkhonto we Sizwe (commonly referred to as MK). In this chapter, we question the history of MK military veterans as a distinct media scarce community whose contributions to the end of the apartheid regime have been sparsely represented by film and media and other stories of the anti-apartheid struggle. MK veterans have lived relatively media scarce lives in the shadow of the media abundant figure of Nelson Mandela and the ANC. Many combatants lived precarious underground lives and assumed other identities so as to avoid identification, capture, or assassination by apartheid-era police and security forces. Subsequently, the goal of the chapter is to discuss the various forms in which MK veterans communicated their covert struggles and ultimately their contributions to the end of apartheid. In lieu of typical propaganda campaigns that use media to communicate goals, ideologies, and misdirections, MK's media scarce politics focused on developing a clandestine communications system, a means of avoiding detection by South African security services. While successful, such media scarce forms of resistance were decommissioned after the end of apartheid, along with legions of armed MK fighters and underground operatives. Today, as many MK veterans enter retirement age, their past media scarce lives have posed new challenges. How can the media scarce veterans communicate their past to advocate for a better future for themselves? The chapter notes in conclusion that only recently have some veterans themselves – through life-story projects, books, and other collaborations – started to fully articulate and understand their own roles and identities in the struggle against apartheid.

Chapter 3 explores the media scarcity of incarcerated populations by challenging the common conception that prisons are structured by a media or digital divide. Although prisons are typically imagined as technologically sparse or empty, they are in fact significant spaces of technological innovation and experimentation (Kaun and Stiernstedt 2020). By contrast, the framework of a divide suggests a gap between the incarcerated and media. We argue rather that carceral power systematically controls media to oppressively structure the storytelling and communicative agency of incarcerated individuals and groups, committing ongoing harms and injustices while also obstructing collective pathways for commiseration and decarceration. The chapter argues that the divisiveness of prison media and communications should be reimagined and refashioned into a *track* – a counter-political infrastructure that can guide the work needed to enact media scarce politics founded on anticolonial principles. We explore one articulation of this path forward through an analysis of Cheryl L'Hirondelle's *Why the Caged Bird Sings* (2015), a nêhiyawin (Cree worldview) song writing collaboration with primarily incarcerated Indigenous women in Canada. L'Hirondelle's work remediates the disciplinary infrastructure of prison visitation, prison libraries, various entertainment media, payphones, and social media into a track of healing and collective wayfinding. We refer to this project as a *ceremonial infrastructure* that brings incarcerated individuals together but also expands the possibilities for public allyship with media scarce struggles.

Chapter 4 focuses on Soviet-era secret, closed or nuclear cities, spaces that were purposefully made media scarce by security restrictions limiting the media documentation of everyday life. The chapter discusses two art-photograph projects that document contemporary images of former cold war-era secret cities. While one set of photographs, captured by Gregor Sailer, depict secret cities devoid of human subjects, others collaboratively produced by Sergey Novikov and former secret city citizens satirically re-stage their memories of a media scarce life for the camera. While subtly critical of media scarce policies in secret cities, Novikov's photos also highlight how they were embraced by many residents. Media scarcity, in other words, sheltered residents of secret cities from the many harsh realities of Soviet life. Since media use was highly regulated in secret cities, their use easily identified non-residents, amplifying the economic and social security experienced by secret city citizenry. Novikov's collaborative project though also highlights the social paranoia, xenophobia, and the economic and environmental toxicity of secret cities after the fall of the Soviet Union. Such cities would later continue to remain relatively media scarce as they shifted from one economic model to the next, experimenting with secretive health care research (on irradiated populations), and then tax-free zones that actively recruited corrupt businesses by sheltering money laundering enterprises.

In Chapter 5, the cold war bunker returns. Unlike the previous chapters, this chapter argues that the cold war bunker represented a globalized media scarce condition, where populations were encouraged to seek shelter underground. Yet while the bunker mirrored the media scarce conditions of many other communities discussed in our book, it was initially sold as an extension of the family home, replete with the creature comforts of the time – notably consumer media technologies. However, the chapter details how this mythic media abundant bunker gave way to militarized bunker visions that emphasized the installation's redundant qualities. Not only would the state bunker contain layers of redundant media technologies in case of attack or technological failure, but the cold war bunker would also never be used for its intended purpose of protection against nuclear arms. Focusing on the case of the

Canadian "continuity of government" bunker located outside of the national capital Ottawa, the chapter concludes with an analysis of the contemporary return of the media abundant bunker, or bunker media, an event hall, and Cold War Museum that once again attempts to keep the precarity of its apocalyptic media scarcity at bay. Instead of nuclear annihilation, the newly refashioned bunker turns to zombies and spy games to remediate and placate the existential cold war threats of an uncertain future in and beyond the underground.

In our concluding chapter 6, we draw parallels from our conceptualization of media scarcity to begin dialogue with key thinkers and concepts to better understand how media reinforces and shapes political divisions and hegemonic political structures. Media is not exempt from power relations. While we noted in our introduction how some writers believe that media is seemingly autonomous from material or economic forms of scarcity, we argue that examples of the homeless or refugees using mobile media (Boczkowski 2021, xi) merely reaffirm the very life-dependent status of media devices and media content today. That is, that struggles over media scarcity can be a matter of life and death. The end goal of these arguments is to align the critiques of media abundances and scarcities – and their relative degrees and political contexts – to other anticolonial efforts, artistic and community-based projects, and media paradigms that emphasize negotiating and refashioning media power as central components of social justice work.

Bibliography

Andrejevic, Mark. 2013. *Infoglut: How Too Much Information Is Changing the Way We Think and Know*. New York: Routledge.
Bastani, Aaron. 2019. *Fully Automated Luxury Communism: A Manifesto*. London: Verso.
Bellamy, Edward. 1888. *Looking Backward, 2000–1887*. Toronto: W. Bryce.
Benjamin, Ruha. 2018. "Black AfterLives Matter." *Boston Review*. Accessed October 19, 2023. https://www.bostonreview.net/articles/ruha-benjamin-black-afterlives-matter/.
Billard, Sebastien, and Hanna Duggal. 2022. "Infographic: Where Is Press Freedom Restricted?" *Aljazeera*. Accessed October 19, 2023. https://www.aljazeera.com/news/2022/5/3/infographic-where-is-press-freedom-restricted-interative.
Boczkowski, Pablo J. 2021. *Abundance: On the Experience of Living in a World of Information Plenty*. Oxford: Oxford University Press.
Borumand, Safura. 2018. "Cornucopia: Origins, Diffusion and Adoption in Ancient Irano-Indian Semiosphere." *Studies in People's History* 5 (2): 166–179.
Browne, Simone. 2015. *Dark Matters: On the Surveillance of Blackness*. Durham: Duke University Press.
Bruns, Axel. 2019. *Are Filter Bubbles Real*. London: Polity.
Brunton, Finn, and Helen Nissenbaum. 2015. *Obfuscation: A User's Guide for Privacy and Protest*. Cambridge: MIT Press.
Craig, Alexander. 1898. *Ionia Land of Wise Men and Fair Women*. Chicago: E.A. Weeks Co.
Croteau, David. 2007. "The Growth of Self-Produced Media Content and the Challenge to Media Studies." *Critical Studies in Media Studies* 23 (4): 340–344.

Cummings, B. 2014. "Encyclopaedic Erasmus." *Renaissance Studies* 28 (2): 183–204. https://doi.org/10.1111/rest.12049.
Daft, Richard. L., and Robert H. Lengel. 1986. "Organizational Information Requirements, Media Richness and Structural Design." *Management Science* 32 (5): 554–571.
"Definition of abundance." 2023. Merriam-Webster. Accessed October 19, 2023. https://www.merriam-webster.com/dictionary/abundance.
Esetena. 2010, June 9. Buscando los restos de las primeras fuentes barrocas (5): la Abundancia. Accessed October 20, 2022. https://www.pasionpormadrid.com/.
Gitelman, Lisa. 2014. *Paper Knowledge: Toward a Media History of Documents.* Durham: Duke University Press.
Hegeler, Edward C. 1911. "The Fish as a Mystic Symbol in China and Japan." *The Open Court* XXV (7): 385–411.
Jenkins, Henry, Sam Ford, and Joshua Green. 2013. *Spreadable Media: Creating Value and Meaning in a Networked Culture.* New York: NYU Press.
Karppinen, Kari. 2009. *Rethinking Media Pluralism and Communicative Abundance.* McGannon Communication Research Center, New York City: Fordham University Press.
Kaun, Anne, and Fredrik Stiernstedt. 2020. "Doing Time, the Smart Way? Temporalities of the Smart Prison." *New Media & Society* 22 (9): 1580–1599.
Keane, John. 2014. *Democracy and Media Decadence.* Cambridge: Cambridge University Press.
Kerr, Ian, Valerie Steeves, and Carole Lucock. 2009. *Lessons from the Identity Trail: Anonymity, Privacy and Identity in a Networked Society.* Oxford: Oxford University Press.
L'Hirondelle, Cheryl. 2015. "Why the Caged Bird Sings: Radical Inclusivity, Sonic Survivance and the Collective Ownership of Freedom Songs." Masters, OCAD University. https://openresearch.ocadu.ca/id/eprint/287/.
Mann, Steve, and Joseph Ferenbok. 2013. "New Media and the Power Politics of Sousveillance in a Surveillance-Dominated World." *Surveillance & Society* 11 (1/2): 18–34.
Manovich, Lev. 2002. *The Language of New Media.* Cambridge: MIT Press.
Milligan, Ian. 2013. *History in the Age of Abundance?* Montreal: McGill-Queens University Press.
Pasquale, Frank. 2015. *The Black Box Society: The Secret Algorithms that Control Money and Information.* Cambridge: Harvard University Press.
Tarde, Gabriel de. 1905. *Underground Man.* Translated by Cloudesley Brereton. London: Duckworth. https://archive.org/details/undergroundman00tard.
Tarde, Gabriel. 2013. *Les Lois de L'Imitation, Etude Sociologique.* Madrid: HardPress Publishing.
"User-Generated Internet Content per Minute 2022." 2022. Statista. Accessed October 19, 2023. https://www.statista.com/statistics/195140/new-user-generated-content-uploaded-by-users-per-minute/.
Wells, Herbert George. 1905. "Preface." In *Underground Man*, edited by Gabriel de Tarde. London: Duckworth. https://archive.org/details/undergroundman00tard.
Williams, James. 2018. *Stand out of Our Light: Freedom and Resistance in the Attention Economy.* Cambridge: Cambridge University Press.

2 Media scarcity in apartheid South Africa

In the spring and summer of 2018, members of South Africa's Umkhonto we Sizwe Military Veterans Association conducted a series of protests to call attention to their lack of housing and employment opportunities. At one such protest, veterans succeeded in occupying and ultimately closing Durban's city hall. A local newspaper noted that "The protesters were in a no-nonsense mood … and displayed open hostility to people taking pictures of them" (Magubane 2018).

Unlike the African National Congress (ANC), which would later become the governing party of South Africa, the party's military wing "Umkhonto we Sizwe" or "Spear of the Nation" (MK for short) disbanded after the end of apartheid. Through interviews with former members, Janet Cherry (2012) estimated that there were two hundred and fifty initial MK members in 1961, "…organized into units of three to four members…under a regional command structure" (17). The organization was parsed into "…cells to avoid detection and…operated on a need-to-know basis" (Ellis 2013, 23). For security reasons, many MK militants lived underground, media scarce lives. Media documentation of an individual's role in the armed resistance could have easily led to detection by the South African security police and likely imprisonment, or worse.

Many MK recruits spent years training in terrible conditions in military camps in the frontline states of Southern Africa waiting to play their part in a liberating armed struggle that ultimately never transpired (Simpson 2016). Cherry (reminds us that those MK members who died of illness and in skirmishes with the security forces in and outside of South Africa "…are no longer publicly remembered. This kind of history always raises controversial issues around who is remembered and how: who was a hero, who a perpetrator, who a martyr and who a victim?" (2012, 129–130). The media scarce nature of MK veterans thus stands in stark contrast to the media rich and visually iconic history of Nelson Mandela (Olesen 2015) and the ANC's post-apartheid visual campaign to merge its history into a future governing narrative for the country (Coombes 2003).

DOI: 10.4324/9781003398639-2

Indeed, the formation of MK was itself purposefully and performatively "undocumented". After ANC leaders voted to initiate military operations against the South African state, the resolution was "...dramatically burned... and the ashes scattered. The resulting decision was officially described as a 'secret' one...It was the real starting point of Umkhonto we Sizwe" (Ellis 2013, 17). Nelson Mandela was initially MK commander, while rank and file members were drawn from the ANC and the Communist Party of South Africa (Ellis and Sechaba 1992, 32). Cherry characterized these first members as "...a small group of saboteurs of all races..." (2012, 17) Later, after the ANC decided to focus on "...strategic targets for sabotage and to avoid casualties as far as possible" (33), the party distanced Mandela and other ANC leaders from MK military tactics, operations, and outcomes. The military wing of the party needed to be seen at least to be a separate entity, with different leaders, and secretive goals and operations. This separation served several purposes, some political (particularly as Nelson Mandela and the ANC negotiated an end to apartheid), and others security minded, as a means to protect the identities of MK members who engaged in undercover and underground operations. Portions of MK's first manifesto make clear this opaque relationship between political organizations, parties, and resistance fighters:

> It is, however, well known that the main national liberation organisations in this country have consistently followed a policy of non-violence. They have conducted themselves peaceably at all times, regardless of government attacks and persecutions upon them, and despite all government-inspired attempts to provoke them to violence. They have done so because the people prefer peaceful methods of change to achieve their aspirations without the suffering and bitterness of civil war. But the people's patience is not endless.
>
> The time comes in the life of any nation when there remain only two choices: submit or fight.
>
> ("Manifesto of Umkhonto We Sizwe" 1961)

The contrast between a media rich ANC and its high-profile leader and media scarce military veterans has only grown since the armed struggle was suspended – part of the negotiated agreement to end apartheid rule in August 1990. Cherry notes in her book *Spear of the Nation* (2012) that MK cadres "...found it hard to accept that their leaders were insisting on a negotiated settlement" (116).

> Instead of returning as heroes, able to meet expectations of their loved ones, they became a burden on their already struggling families...the joy at finally going back home was tempered in many cases by confusion and disorientation. By the end of 1992, some MK returnees were protesting at

the ANC headquarters because of their dissatisfaction with the way they were being treated.

(122)

Unlike many other decolonial struggles throughout Africa, white minority rule ended after political negotiations – a process that further displaced the role played by MK, both at the time and years later.

We begin our book with the case of MK operatives, some soldiers, others organizers, and underground operatives, to highlight the historical forms of media scarce storytelling, in particular noting its persistence in the post-apartheid era. Moreover, the MK example adds further specificity and definition to our notion of *scarcity in abundance*, as an secretive underground group that operated in the shadow of the media savvy and abundant ANC. We highlight two particular media scarce strategies adopted by MK and its members. We argue, first, that acting in the shadow of the ANC, MK adopted an infrastructural form of media scarce politics. Specifically, MK repurposed letters and the mail system into a spectacular yet anonymous form of communication design to inspire their supporters while evading and misdirecting the South African apartheid state and police. And second, after the end of apartheid, we discuss a more personal aspect of media scarcity, namely how covert MK members' recollections of their past lives have been hampered by not only being media scarce and *unknown* (by avoiding media to maintain their aliases or "legends" that masked their true identifies and actions); they were also, at the same time themselves *unknowing*, kept in the dark by their comrades and handlers about the role that they played in operations to undermine the apartheid state.

Even today, as we will detail later in the chapter, there is a relative scarcity of MK stories and narratives depicting the armed resistance, again particularly when compared with the ANC's role in fighting apartheid. MK storytelling is a secretive, underground form of storytelling, one that has an uneasy relationship with media capture, as evidenced in the protesting MK veterans' aversion to being photographed. But media scarce storytelling, communication, and advocacy are not solely defined by the absence of media documentation or a refusal to be documented. Rather this persistence of media scarcity well beyond the apartheid decades itself tells a story – it reveals efforts to speak, protest, and advocate about silences, undocumented experiences, and covert operations, lives, and identities.

We begin then by asking how MK members communicated a secretive, media scarce struggle, during and after apartheid, with seemingly little media or, later, historical media documentation. For this chapter, we pay particular attention to the anti-apartheid struggles of the 1980s,[1] when MK engaged in underground operations within South Africa itself with the help of militants from the townships and allies from around the world. We analyse how their covert underground operations informed their media scarce form of storytelling and politics. This past media scarcity is made all the more urgent given the shifting media landscape that MK veterans face today, where the sharing of social media objects and documents has become decidedly *overt*, a common daily practice (Jurgenson 2019) and essential practice in contemporary political campaigns (Chadwick 2013). In contrast to the image heavy and discrete media objects that are shared on social media platforms and throughout the media industries, the chapter details how MK engaged in an underground and clandestine form of media infrastructure work, building the capacity to undermine and question the legitimacy of the violent apartheid regime. While part of this media work integrated coded forms of communication, it also embraced media scarcity, leaving behind little documentation or traces of MK identities.

In the latter half of the chapter, we see how this "protective" form of media scarcity continues to this very day, with MK veterans struggling to remember, perform, sketch, or otherwise communicate the precarious conditions of their past underground lives and ultimately their own identities, "legends", and operational contributions to the end of apartheid. Our focus on performative, historical documentation of MK lives, memories, and experiences is in part inspired by Rebecca Schreiber's *The Undocumented Everyday: Migrant Lives and the Politics of Visibility* (2018), Sarah Bishop's *Undocumented Storytellers: Narrating the Immigrant Rights Movement* (2019), and other research on forced migration and media. We believe that such projects offer an important corrective to the predominant "abundant" theories of media today, guided by a culture of social media sharing deemed essential to cultivating public recognition and personal reputations. By comparison in this and subsequent chapters, we analyse how the undocumented and media scarce engage in a form of mediated politics of recognition, celebration, and community building.

Media infrastructure as armed propaganda

Historically, MK and their international supporters left the anti-apartheid media campaign to the ANC's exiled leadership. But this didn't mean they avoided mediated politics altogether, particularly after the ANC adopted a new strategy to mobilize the masses in the struggle and resistance against apartheid within South Africa. The new military policy – articulated in yet another secretive document that was only read by a selective few leaders (the "Green book") – would by 1981 usher in

> Armed propaganda…a form of spectacular attacks…The purpose of such attacks was not so much to damage the South African war machine as to inform South Africa and the world that Umkhonto we Sizwe was in business…Armed propaganda was also intended to attract new recruits.
> (Ellis 2013, 128)

Going forward, this shift in policy placed greater emphasis on informal networks of underground and undercover MK operatives, backed by secretly embedded fighters in border states.

Prior to the armed propaganda campaign, media scarcity had always been a factor in the operations of MK and the lives of its members, indeed dating back to its secretive founding. Communication among cadres, fighters, ANC leaders, and overseas supporters was always haphazard, unstable, insecure, and dangerous. In other words, MK operatives and fighters always faced obstacles to communication, both with central command and with each other, again because they were constantly under threat of detection by the apartheid state. Communications and media documentation meant potential identification, as a medium through which MK fighters and operatives could be targeted and operations disrupted. Guerrilla fighters as a group of course are defined against a centralized and organized group or government. As a consequence, MK guerilla fighters and underground operatives were tasked with establishing de-centred, yet coordinated forms of communication, often as core elements of their missions. In short, MK operatives served as militants and infrastructure workers, establishing a "media scarce" system of communications that would be undetectable by the apartheid state.[2]

MK's deployment of letter bombs and dead letter drops served as key components in their media scarce communications infrastructure, an anonymous system designed to mask the identities and location of MK operatives. MK letters could not be channelled through the regular postal system, with addresses meant to locate and identify authors and readers. MK's dead letters became purposefully hidden and masked forms of communication since there was no central communication system. Dead letter drops served as underground nodes in a precarious media environment, a media scarce tactic – they served as sites of resistance to media capture and identification. The technique, however, was not new. Dead letter boxes served as important nodes in clandestine communications networks during the cold war. Some MK leaders and operatives were trained by East German Stasi officers during the height of the struggle against apartheid (Ellis 2013). Operatives learned to camouflage dead letter drops and boxes as other media objects, often as pens or other discarded everyday objects, like empty cigarette boxes. Covert MK recruits were also schooled in the art of using invisible ink (Ahern 2012, 137). Communications and arms were placed in boxes and stored in locations where other MK operatives would later retrieve them. Such dead drops or boxes thus served to protect against operatives – or the content of boxes – being captured. These were media scarce military objects and short form, coded forms of communication, that if found would mask or misdirect their true meaning and intent. Moreover, taken as a whole, dead letter boxes effectively served as a network of communications that coordinated the movement of arms and other clandestine equipment.

Letters would also become a key symbolic weapon in MK's post-1979 campaign of armed propaganda. In addition to serving as nodes in a media scarce communication network, letters were also designed and synchronized to explode – and communicate. Letter bomb campaigns were used by MK as synchronized forms of communication, a powerful expression of coordinated action – a literally weaponized communications network or explosive burst of communicative resistance. One international MK recruit summarized his role in one such campaign succinctly: "I had become an underground 'postman' from another world" (Schechter 2012, 54). Central to the campaign was the deployment of a series of letter bombs stuffed inside innocuous looking briefcases, a hybrid communication/weapon that required a coordinated system of activation. Similar efforts to synchronize public speeches on busy city streets used hidden cassette tape players. Coordination was key as synchronized explosions of leaflets communicated to both the apartheid state and the townships that an active resistance was organized and dispersed throughout the country. Coordinated letter bombs also provided a distraction from other covert activities that required cover within the borders of apartheid South Africa. Ken Keable (2012) explains:

> ...Our action was designed to draw police resources into the cities and away from the townships for a while, thus leaving the townships relatively free for the ANC members there to carry out other activities which would normally be too dangerous.
>
> (35)

Naturally, as a consequence of the clandestine nature of the MK fight against apartheid, operatives had to constantly avoid detection and refrain from documenting their actual roles in operations or more broadly the fight against the South African security agencies. In this context, it should come as no surprise that written texts, in the form of letters, emerged as a central node in coded communications (Toupin 2016) and in the deployment of a propaganda war against apartheid. In lieu of conducting a multi-mediated propaganda war then (films, videos, photography), MK leaders developed informal networks of communication among underground operatives that working in cells operationalized dead letter boxes and synchronized letter bombs. The media scarce battle against apartheid, in other words, was in part a battle conducted through infrastructure and spectacle – an effort to communicate from the underground.

Media strategies: overcoming media scarcity

Synchronized MK letter bombs are well-documented elements of a story of organized resistance and struggle, but what about the lives of MK members themselves, the images or sounds from their past experiences as underground militants? In addition to avoiding media, coding, hiding, or camouflaging their communications, the true nature and scope of operations that they participated in were also hidden. MK operatives were unknown and unknowing. Individual underground operatives, in other words, were largely kept in the dark about the broader goals of MK operations – while operatives hid their opinions, identities, and operations, they were also shielded from knowing their own roles in the larger struggle. Since decommissioning and the end of apartheid, however, MK operatives and their allies have begun to piece together their roles in this secretive network of resistance.

Pictures hand drawn from memories have played an important role in MK storytelling, both during the conflict and after the fall of apartheid. The hand-drawn image is almost synonymous with clandestine, media scarce life. The drawing of a map or contact information on the back of a napkin or inside of a cigarette box always presages its disposal (or accidental discovery!). Other media scarce communities, including the incarcerated, detained, and imprisoned (which we discuss in Chapter 3), have also drawn heavily upon hand-drawn images to communicate their media scarce experiences behind bars. Tings Chak's *Undocumented: The Architecture of Migrant Detention* (2014) is but one compelling, yet unconventional book that contains sketches from memories of the incarcerated – images that depict the brutal loneliness, architectural violence, and injustice of detention spaces. O'Neill and Fogarty-Valenzuela (2020), similarly, highlight artistic projects used to communicate the experiences of media scarce, incarcerated lives. Influenced by "the albums produced by Russian soldiers, concentration camp inmates, and people who experienced the siege of Leningrad" (8), Victoria Lomasko's (2017) celebrated drawings of Russian lives though are more befitting the case of MK operatives. Through a distinct form of "life drawing", Lomasko argues that the subjects of her drawings are not only "invisible" to the world but also to themselves (7). We return to this point in our concluding section that discusses MK "legends", of their being "unknown" political actors, to the apartheid state or indeed their "unknowing" selves.

Ken Keable's (2012) collection of personal MK testimonies and memories, arguably the first in a line of recent publications to have opened the door for former MK operatives to learn more about their past lives and their comrades, begins with a hand-drawn sketch of a bag that contained a leaflet bomb, including all the technical elements (time switch, wires) and a "Toy spider (or snake) to deter inquisitive people" (v). Such aesthetics can in part be traced back to MK's few publications, most notably the monthly newsletter *Dawn: Journal of Umkhonto we Sizwe* (1977–1988)[3] which consistently published hand-drawn images on its cover, a sun on the masthead, and typically spears and other similar weaponry in its table of contents.[4] Apart from such hand-drawn images, the entire series of publications is overwhelmingly text based, clearly produced on a typewriter. Again, what few MK media exist conform to our scarcity in abundance thesis – MK had to remain anonymous and underground, abstractly sketched not photographed. In *Dawn*, MK faces are absent. Take for example the "Souvenir Issue" celebrating the anniversary of 25th Anniversary of MK, which includes a large unedited photo of the young Robben Island prisoner Nelson Mandela. Like many contemporary books on the MK, the issue includes photos of ANC and MK leaders but uses hand-drawn images of cadres to represent the masses of MK fighters. One such drawing depicts a cadre with raised fist holding a Kalashnikov rifle, the iconic weapon of anti-imperialist fighters of the time. The rifle is also a constant in MK posters celebrating various MK anniversaries ("The Racists Shall Not Rule" 1986).

MK posters similarly deployed hand-drawn do-it-yourself (DIY) like images that are more reminiscent of punk rock concert promotions than political communiques in an armed struggle. Some posters can still be found today for sale on internet poster stores. One such site offers a choice of four DIY like posters of the MK martyr Solomon Mahlangu ("Umkhonto Wesizwe Mk Posters for Sale" n.d.). Another heavily stylized MK poster by a South African designer Tristan Vogt offers a more contemporary representation of MK,[5] with abstract guns emerging out of a masked figure in a forest of cacti (Vogt 2011). The most common motif in most drawings – and through the sparse publications and posters from MK – is the Zulu warrior, a near mythic figure that represents opposition to British Colonialism in South Africa (Laband 2014). A hand-drawn Zulu-like figure with oval shield and spear for example adorns the masthead of *Dawn*. The use of hand drawn spears is also prevalent throughout *Dawn* and on MK posters produced for distribution to the townships beginning in 1980 ("20 Years of Action!" n.d.). It is only later in the 1980s as the end of apartheid approached that MK posters began to consistently incorporate images of popular uprisings with the recognizable green, yellow, and black colour scheme of the ANC ("Forward to freedom" n.d.).

Life stories and MK testimonials

Besides a select number of documentary films that commonly stage re-enactments,[6] the other main medium of media scarce MK history is the testimonial. Indeed, MK testimonials and memories are often used to narrate re-enacted scenes in documentary film. Testimonials also served as the key medium through which South Africa emerged out of the bitter apartheid era – in the form of the truth and reconciliation process that witnessed harrowing personal accounts of the devastating impact of decades of racist policies, police torture, and armed struggle ("Truth and Reconciliation Commission Report" 1998). In sum, these testimonials were designed as a broader media strategy in support of post-apartheid civil society, as an attempt to put behind the many years of secrecy, covert operations, and state sanctioned discrimination and violence. While personal stories told to the Truth and Reconciliation Commission served to recognize past injustices, common grief, and hopes for a peaceful future, critics have also noted its narrow and focused role in legitimizing the new post-apartheid, multiracial state. Fullard and Rousseau (2008), for example, write:

> ....The most compelling criticism of the TRC has been the way in which its mandate penned a characterisation of political violence that excluded the structural violence of apartheid. The mandate painted a narrow definition of gross human rights violations, confining its gaze to the physical and repressive dimensions of apartheid rule that occurred in direct political repression and conflict, rather than the structural and everyday violence of apartheid.
>
> (225)

In contrast to documentary cinema and, to some extent, the proceedings of the TRC, MK testimonies have, for the past decade, begun to address the "everyday" gap in media scarce storytelling – stories about the personal everyday lived experiences of underground operatives. While biographies and autobiographies of MK leaders such as Chris Hani (Dam and Tromp 2010; MacMillan 2018) and Ronnie Kasrils (1993) have received book-length attention going back to the early 1990s, rank and file MK operatives have only recently started to narrate their own underground and clandestine experiences. Unlike these MK leadership profiles and histories, the stories told in edited collections by Gunn and Haricharan's *Voices from the Underground* (2019), Keable's aforementioned *London Recruits* (2012), and Kasrils's *International Brigade Against Apartheid* (2021) are brief, tentative, and often modest. A number of Kasril's contributors used pseudonyms, while the editor also noted how some MK veterans refused to participate in the book project. Some MK authors who did participate wrote of being scared to tell their stories, still fearing reprisal more than thirty years after the end of apartheid.

Like the book-length biographies of MK leadership, rank and file MK stories often exhibit a common narrative form, what Paul Gready (2003) refers to as "life stories". Gready argues that such autobiographical life stories are particularly relevant to the personal experiences of anti-apartheid activists and exiles. To that end, he argues that "The aim of the life story in such a context, after all, is to proclaim a self in the face of its official destruction and denial…they provide a window between apartheid as ideology and as lived experience" (9). The life story is therefore, in part, a media scarce form of storytelling, a coming to terms with a largely unmediated, undocumented, clandestine life. In addition to articulating the early predispositions for joining the dangerous, underground battle against apartheid, Gready also argues that such life stories necessarily seek to negotiate and understand past "…events, situations, moral choices, and lives that were 'half told' and 'half known'…" (10). As a consequence, a key aspect of media scarce storytelling among MK operatives has been a struggle to define and articulate a singular identity or experience. And yet, in the end, as Gready observes, "identity essentialism... was undercut by the need for selves and narratives to be flexible, provisional, tactical, inventive, and un/remade, to be managed in order to take up their appointed time and place on the narrative and political battlefield" (10).

Central to the discomfort, reticence and "flexibility" of media scarce MK storytelling and life stories was – and remains – their operational "legends", a term used to connote a cover story and identity "...to screen their movements and behaviour" (Kasrils 2021, 18). The term *legend* is, however, more commonly used to refer to commanding, "larger than life" figures, such as the media abundant ANC leadership. Yet throughout MK life stories in recent edited collections, operatives describe their legends as crucial components of their media scarce life avoiding identification and capture. Legends served as plausible stories that didn't require fulsome – or moreover truthful – documentation. And that part of cultivating and rehearsing their legends was the need to destroy any existing media documents of their political identities as MK and ANC supporters and operatives. One operative wrote about destroying all her diaries (Raadschelders 2012, 315), while others discussed how they were given books by their handlers without a personal dedication. Keable writes: "I kept nothing by way of a souvenir of my exploit, or any physical evidence, as I didn't feel safe from the possibility of investigation even at home" (2012, 30).

MK legends then were not iconic images or mythic stories that actively told and retold "a story coming down from the past" ("Definition of legend" 2023). Throughout the MK book collections, some operatives refer to legends as plausible cover stories (including their daily jobs), while others used the term more personally, in reference to their fake names and persona. Some legends were decidedly granular, impromptu, and improvised cover stories meant to quickly provide plausible alternative explanations to security forces and police. One MK veteran, for example, wrote about digging a hole to hide a cache of weapons in a remote location by the side of the road: "Once the then feared South African Police stopped next to my car and peered through the bushes in my direction as I nervously clutched my Swiss Army Knife and toilet roll (Hint: what the hole could be used for.)" (Garraway 2012, 114). Likewise most legends, as plausible stories, helped to provide cover for short visits to South Africa from outside the country, often by white international supporters, recruited because of their ability to pass the scrutiny of the racist South African security and border agencies. One MK operative wrote: "We travelled as wealthy tourists, not scruffy students" (Milotte 2012, 96), others posed as newlyweds on their honeymoon (Levine 2012, 108)

To mirror Gready's points about life stories, these media scarce "legends" were more than plausible lies, but carefully crafted to make sense to the South African authorities. Legends also reflected real experiences, embodied and lived truths, as reflected in the life stories told by many MK operatives. Operatives often described how beautiful their trip was, using tourist-like language – for example, how Cape Town was an "idyllic holiday place" (Levine 2012, 111). Others conducted operations in Joburg then retreated to a more obvious tourist experience in Durban before returning to their home countries: "Everyday we went to the glorious beaches" (Whyte 2012, 257).

Yet for those MK veterans who made longer term commitments, their legends were more complex, difficult to maintain, and psychologically taxing. Their legends were personal, reflecting the years spent acting as another person. As Kasrils notes: "These volunteers asked for nothing in compensation. They did not receive salaries; and were in most cases dependent on finding jobs to make ends meet and provide the necessary cover they required" (2022, 17). As a consequence, many longer term MK operatives found jobs that were also meant to hide or mask their operations and political opinions. Many MK operatives who assisted in border states, by providing communications and often arms to cross the border into South Africa, worked as teachers, educators, or development workers. But such professional "legends" or cover professions also masked a deeper legend, a cover identity that needed to avoid at all costs being seen to oppose or even have knowledge of the racist operations of the apartheid state.

Unlike most short-term MK operatives, these embedded "legends" had to manage and maintain masked identities over many years. Theirs was not a tourist lifestyle or social one. Many operatives wrote of the isolation and loneliness that underground and undercover life produced. One operative wrote:

> We had to be well aware and prepared, politically and psychologically... Never to let your guard down. Always to be that other *persona*...You don't get used to life in the underground. You shouldn't. Because if you do, then that could be fatal. Every step you take must be considered being under observation, every innocent action being scrutinised by suspicious eyes, every phone call considered reaching listening ears...Paranoia and suspicion feed on themselves. Just like depression. The life we lived was a life of isolation and stress.
>
> (Koster 2012, 119–121)

MK operatives, as a distinct media scarce community, then could perhaps better be described as living legends, as storytellers, in keeping with the definition of legend as a verb, "to tell or narrate" ("Cover Story vs Legend" n.d.).

Conclusions

Personal stories serve as a common starting point for many forms of media scarce communications, whether documentary script, history book, or drawings from a veteran's memory. One exception, however, is MK iconography where popular, mythic, and historic aesthetics served important roles in the media scarce communication strategies of MK veterans and storytellers. Such

DIY-like images served to reinforce a powerful armed resistance –a form of armed propaganda and a creative ingenuity that was designed to inspire common and contagious forms of resistance. Given the secretive, underground life of MK operations and lives of its members, however, it should come as no surprise that mediated interventions or spectacles served as key sites and tactics of the armed propaganda campaign. Such synchronized events, the letter bomb campaigns, remind us of the importance of performance in media scarce communities, be they re-enactments or other creative expressions of common experiences. To this end, we have also seen that media scarcity for the MK involved developing a corresponding, distributed, and secure form of communication, a media scarce communications infrastructure specifically designed to distract, confuse, and camouflage the goals of MK.

Media campaigns and mediated histories of media scarce communities and individuals are complex and multifaceted phenomena that interface with a series of political and personal circumstances and agendas in South Africa and around the world. As previously noted, media scarcity is not restricted to former MK underground fighters and agents – the term could apply to any community that has sought to avoid media capture or who have lost all or some of their possessions, including media archives. As a consequence, these communities may lack official documentation that is required to access services and rights. But in the case of MK veterans, we have also seen that media scarcity, or lacking media documents and histories, has often led to infrastructure building and spectacular events, designed to communicate strength, resolve, and a persistent resistance to oppression and injustice. Yet as the years have passed, MK's media scarce communication and storytelling strategies remain difficult, brief, and perceived as still precarious. MK media scarcity is constituted and contested by not only the lack of media history and documentation but also a lack of knowledge, an individual and collective self-knowledge, a knowledge of its own secret past, and, most frustratingly, a full understanding of MK contributions to the end of the apartheid state.

With a new generation of post-apartheid citizens assuming leadership roles in South Africa, coupled with an ageing MK veteran population, the task of communicating media scarce experiences continues to be a media scarce challenge. The high-profile nature of the ANC always and already put MK in its shadow, a scarcity in abundance that complicates veteran's present-day appeals and advocacy. MK though have produced and mobilized media artefacts on their own terms and from their own unique histories in the struggle against apartheid. Some of these artifacts have been updated, adopted, and mobilized as digital media objects, as we have seen with regard to the image of the Zulu warrior, while other more nuanced treatments of South African history in cinema have also begun to emerge. The voice of MK operatives, however, remains relatively elusive, in search of social justice – especially the knowing and known voice, the voice and experience of the legends in the struggle against apartheid.

Notes

1 This period marks the beginning of the end of apartheid rule in South Africa.
2 The quasi-memoir of Tim Jenkin (1995), for instance, outlines his role in developing a coded communications network for the ANC during operation VULA. Jenkin's work also serves as a point of departure for Toupin's (2016) theory of Jenkin and other ANC operatives as communications hackers.
3 *Dawn* was largely circulated to MK exiles outside of South Africa (Longford 2022).
4 Research has also begun to emerge on the use of poetry by female MK members. For example, Kebotlhale Motseothata (2022) recently wrote that "…poems serve as an archive of women's individual and collective thinking about their role in the liberation struggle….[they] provide a window into the collective thoughts and struggles of rank and file MK members, including its women… the poetry published in *Dawn* played a role in not only the mobilisation and resistance against apartheid, but also in the ways in which MK women soldiers exercised their agency and envisioned their role in the struggle, as well as in the future South Africa. In reading their poetry, we are invited to imagine the affective dimensions of their lives in the struggle, where the personal is political".
5 https://dribbble.com/shots/1526444-uMkhonto-weSizwe-Poster
6 Namely *MK – The People's Army* (1993, Dir. Zeph R. Makgetla), *The Secret Safari* (2001, Dir. Tom Zubrycki), *The Luthuli Detachment* (2007, Dir. Zolile ka Nqose), and *The Vula Connection* (2014, Dir. Marion Edmunds).

Bibliography

Ahern, Daniel. 2012. "Of Boats and Borders." In *London Recruits: The Secret War Against Apartheid*, edited by John Keable, 132–146. London: Merlin.
Bishop, Sarah C. 2018. *Undocumented Storytellers: Narrating the Immigrant Rights Movement.* Oxford: Oxford University Press.
Chadwick, Andrew. 2013. *The Hybrid Media System: Politics and Power.* Oxford: Oxford University Press.
Chak, Tings. 2014. *Undocumented: The Architecture of Migrant Detention.* Montreal: The Architectural Observer.
Cherry, Janet. 2012. *Spear of the Nation: Umkhonto weSizwe: South Africa's Liberation Army, 1960s–1990s*, 1st edition. Athens: Ohio University Press.
Coombes, Annie E. 2003. *History After Apartheid: Visual Culture and Public Memory in a Democratic South Africa.* Durham: Duke University Press.
"Cover Story vs Legend: What Is the Difference?" n.d. DiffSense. Accessed October 19, 2023. https://diffsense.com/diff/cover%20story/legend.
Dam, Janet Smith, and Beauregard Tromp. 2010. *Hani A Life Too Short.* Johannesburg: Jonathan Ball Publishers.
Dawn: *Journal of Umkhonto we Sizwe*. 1986. https://disa.ukzn.ac.za/sites/default/files/pdf_files/DaSI86.1681.5785.000.000.1986.pdf.
"Definition of Legend." 2023. Merriam-Webster. https://www.merriam-webster.com/dictionary/legend.
Ellis, Stephen. 2013. *External Mission: The ANC in Exile, 1960–1990.* Oxford: Oxford University Press.
Ellis, Stephen, and Tsepo Sechaba. 1992. *Comrades Against Apartheid: The ANC & the South African Communist Party.* Bloomington: Indiana University Press.

"Forward to Freedom. Victory Is Certain. ANC (South Africa)." n.d. *International Institute of Social History*. Accessed October 19, 2023. https://search.iisg.amsterdam/Record/1144581.

Fullard, Madeleine & Nicky Rousseau. 2008. "Uncertain Borders: The TRC and the (un)Making of Public Myths". Kronos: Journal of Cape History 34: 215–239.

Garraway, James. 2012. "This Is No Picnic, It's War!" In *International Brigade Against Apartheid*, edited by Ronnie Kasrils, 111–115. Wakefield, QC: Daraja.

Gready, Paul. 2003. *Writing as Resistance: Life Stories of Imprisonment, Exile, and Homecoming from Apartheid South Africa*. Lanham: Lexington.

Jenkin, Tim. 1995. "Talking to Vula: The Story of the Secret Underground Communications Network of Operation Vula." *Mayibuye* 6 (3). Archived at http://www.hartford-hwp.com/archives/37a/146.html

Jurgenson, Nathan. 2019. *The Social Photo: On Photography and Social Media*. London: Verso.

Kasrils, Ronnie. 1993. *Armed and Dangerous: My Undercover Struggle Against Apartheid*. Oxford: Heinemann.

Kasrils, Ronnie. 2021. *International Brigade Against Apartheid*. Johannesburg: Jacana Media.

Keable, Ken, ed. 2012. *London Recruits: The Secret War Against Apartheid*. Exeter: Merlin.

Koster, Pierre. 2012. "Of Fish Eagles and DLBs." In *International Brigade Against Apartheid*, edited by Ronnie Kasrils, 116–122. Wakefield, QC: Daraja.

Laband, John. 2014. *Zulu Warriors: The Battle for the South African Frontier*. New Haven: Yale University Press.

Levine, Katherine. 2012. "Untitled." In *London Recruits: The Secret War Against Apartheid*, edited by John Keable, 104–114. London: Merlin.

Lomasko, Victoria. 2017. *Other Russias*. New York: N+1.

Longford. 2022. "Dawn: Sites of Struggle, Contested Historical Narratives and the Making of the Disciplined Cadre." *Revolutionary Papers*. Accessed October 19, 2023. https://revolutionarypapers.org/teaching-tool/dawn/.

Macmillan, Hugh. 2018. *Chris Hani*. Johannesburg: Jacana Media.

Magubane, Thami. 2018. "Protesting MK Vets Close City Hall." Accessed February 4, 2019. https://www.iol.co.za/mercury/protesting-mk-vets-close-city-hall-14231642.

"Manifesto of Umkhonto We Sizwe." 1961. Accessed October 19, 2023. https://www.sahistory.org.za/archive/manifesto-umkhonto-we-sizwe.

Milotte, Mike. 2012. "Working for Ronnie." In *London Recruits: The Secret War Against Apartheid*, edited by John Keable, 93–103. London: Merlin.

Motseothata, Kebotlhale. 2022. "Dawn: Journal of Umkhonto Wa Sizwe." *Revolutionary Papers*. 2022. https://revolutionarypapers.org/journal/dawn-journal-of-umkhonto-wa-sizwe/.

Olesen, Thomas. 2015. "Global Political Iconography: The Making of Nelson Mandela." *American Journal of Cultural Sociology* 3 (1): 34–64.

O'Neill, Kevin Lewis, and Benjamin Fogarty-Valenzuela. 2020. *Art of Captivity/Arte Del Cautiverio*. Toronto: University of Toronto Press.

Raadschelders, Lucia. 2012. "On High Heels." In *London Recruits: The Secret War Against Apartheid*, edited by John Keable, 311–321. London: Merlin.

Schechter, Daniel. 2012. "The Day I Joined the Revolution." In *London Recruits: The Secret War Against Apartheid*, edited by Ken Keable, 51–66. Exeter: Merlin.

Schreiber, Rebecca M. 2018. *The Undocumented Everyday: Migrant Lives and the Politics of Visibility*. Minneapolis: University of Minnesota Press.

Simpson, Thula. 2016. *Umkhonto We Sizwe: The ANC's Armed Struggle*. New York: Penguin.

"The Racists Shall Not Rule. The People Shall Govern. ANC (South Africa)." International Institute of Social History. 1986. Accessed October 19, 2023. https://search.iisg.amsterdam/Record/1144579.

Toupin, Sophie. 2016. "Gesturing Towards Anti-Colonial Hacking and its Infrastructure." *Journal of Peer Production*, #9. Accessed June 24, 2019. http://peerproduction.net/editsuite/issues/issue-9-alternative-internets/peer-reviewed-papers/anti-colonial-hacking/

"Truth and Reconciliation Commission Report." 1998. Government website. Justice and Constitutional Development. Accessed October 19, 2023. https://www.justice.gov.za/trc/report/.

"Umkhonto Wesizwe Mk Posters for Sale." n.d. Redbubble. Accessed October 19, 2023. https://www.redbubble.com/shop/umkhonto+wesizwe+mk+posters.

Vogt, Tristan. 2011. "Umkhonto We Sizwe." DeviantArt. September 6, 2011. Accessed October 19, 2023. https://www.deviantart.com/tristanvogt/art/Umkhonto-We-Sizwe-257035918.

Whyte, Graeme. 2012. "Durban 1971." In *London Recruits: The Secret War Against Apartheid*, edited by John Keeble, 249–265. London: Merlin.

"20 Years of Action! Umkhonto We Sizwe. ANC (South Africa)." n.d. International Institute of Social History. Accessed October 19, 2023. https://search.iisg.amsterdam/Record/1144583.

3 Retracking incarceration
Cheryl L'Hirondelle's ceremonial infrastructure

Hollywood has given us a pervasive image of media scarcity tied to incarceration: After being arrested and booked in jail, you have the right to make a *single* phone call. But what happens when no one picks up? What barriers does this lack of communication and media access raise for the incarcerated beyond the hard fact of cell walls? Carceral environments, be they jails, prisons, or detainment centres, are typically austere spaces marked by minimal furnishings and bland, cold colours. Yet, in addition to this environmental scarcity, prisons are typically also imagined as media scarce institutions, absent of digital media technologies.

Challenging the imaginary of media scarcity in prisons, Kaun and Stiernstedt (2023) introduce the concept of "prison media" to draw attention to the array of media that is produced in and for prison, which includes virtual reality applications, digital games, for both education purposes and escapist role-play (Farley 2018) and various smart prison technologies (Kaun and Stiernstedt 2022). Despite the intensive saturation of media technologies within prisons, the structure and affordances of prison media involve a dual logic of deprivation and extraction. Incarcerated people can be deprived of media and basic communicative rights or rewarded this as a "privilege" for positive behaviour. Yet increasingly, media access in prisons is subtended by intensive surveillance and data extraction. Together, media deprivation and informational extraction function to reproduce the media scarcity of incarcerated individuals, communities, and populations. Discussions of incarcerated populations tend to emphasize how a logic of deprivation produces a "media divide", one that is arguably made more severe within an information age or culture of media abundance (Arguelles and Ortiz-Luis 2021; Jewkes and Johnston 2009; Jewkes and Reisdorf 2016; Van de Steene and Knight 2017). Yet this framing does a poor job in accounting for the saturation of media technologies in prisons and its accompanying extractive logic.

A divide denotes a clear separation, yet it is apparent from the framework of prison media that the dual logic of extraction and deprivation in carceral environments is not a direct result of there being too much or too little media technology. Moreover, a divide typically suggests that those lacking voice must be given access or a platform, and that there is thus a public responsibility to provide and empower the incarcerated with the necessary tools and media – to give "voice to the voiceless'. However, this begs the question: in a contemporary culture of media abundance, would such a shift truly manage to captivate public attention, inspire meaningful reform, and unsettle the contemporary carceral regime?

In recognition of the vital importance of refashioning the conditions of media scarcity for incarcerated individuals and groups, and building upon the work of acclaimed Cree/halfbreed[1] artist, Cheryl L'Hirondelle, we propose to reconceptualize the carceral media *divide* as a *track*. As a noun, a track denotes a course of action or a continuous line, such as the tracks of a railroad. Thus, the track of carceral media scarcity can refer to the infrastructure that continues the objectives of disciplinary institutions while obscuring and obstructing pathways of release, rehabilitation, and carceral reform – in short, pathways of decarceration. Moreover, as a verb, tracking implicates media monitoring and surveillance, as in radar tracking or camera tracking in film, and thus reminds us again of the mediated aspects of incarceration. However, a track can also be imagined as more than the carceral infrastructure of enclosure beyond the strategies of top-down control. Rather a track can be provisional and not firmly constructed, as in a "rough path" or "minor road". In other words, a track can emerge from tactics of resistance (Certeau 1984) as incarcerated individuals and groups contest the conditions of media scarcity, opening a track as a line of struggle for themselves and for others. Crucially, we conceptualize tracks of resistance as pathways that run along and push beyond the divide.

Why the Caged Bird Sings

Cheryl L'Hirondelle's *Why the Caged Bird Sings* is a decades-long collaborative songwriting project undertaken with primarily Indigenous women co-writers in correctional institutions across Canada. Belonging to amiskwaciy wâskahikan (Papaschase First Nation, Edmonton) and Kikino Métis Settlement, Alberta in Canada, L'Hirondelle is a singer-songwriter, interdisciplinary artist, and scholar who brings nêhiyawin (Cree worldview) to critical engagements with music, Indigenous culture, and new media. The project was developed through regular visits by L'Hirondelle to prisons and healing lodges in Canada between 2008 and 2015, collaborating in a spirit of "radical inclusivity" (2015) with Indigenous incarcerated women, men, and youth, in addition to literacy teachers and guards, in order to co-compose and record original songs. The collaboration included a series of sessions where participants co-wrote lyrics and performed and recorded vocals over the course of five days. While formally complete, in every respect *Why the Caged Bird Sings* remains an ongoing project, as L'Hirondelle continues to create new iterations, continuing to correspond with some of her incarcerated collaborators and seeking out formerly incarcerated collaborators online to record their singing voices and register them as copyright holders of the music.

In *Hungry Listening* (2020), xwélmexw (Stó:lō/Skwah) artist and scholar Dylan Robinson relates L'Hirondelle's work to what Wiisaakodewini (Métis) artist Dylan Miner calls a "methodology of visiting" (172). Echoing Anishinaabe elders, Miner expresses his concern that many Indigenous people do not visit one another as frequently as before due to the pressures of urbanization and wage labour, and other effects of settler colonialism (Kisynska 2016). The strain on visiting customs is in many ways obviously compounded for incarcerated Indigenous populations as individuals and communities must navigate restrictive prison visitation and communication policies that fail to accommodate unique cultural and spiritual needs. Still, Indigenous visiting rights in Canada are increasingly being affirmed through Indigenizing initiatives in prisons designed to increase Indigenous programming and supports, as through elder visits and other services (Tetrault 2022). The integration of culturally specific customs of *visiting* into prisons aims to remedy the limitations of a Western model of carceral *visitation* by integrating invaluable aspects of ceremony for incarcerated Indigenous people.

Robinson observes that a methodology of visiting underlies much "Indigenous social arts practice" due to its potential to incite dialogic forms of decolonial action and social change (172–173). However, he cautions that Indigenous enactments of visiting can easily be exploited by Western models of "extractive knowledge gathering" (173), as Indigenous conversations and stories are put on display and evaluated within art exhibitions and curatorial spaces. With this cautionary note in mind, in this chapter we extend Robinson's brief yet insightful reading of *Why the Caged Bird Sings* by exploring how L'Hirondelle navigates carceral infrastructure and the disciplinary policies of media scarcity to refashion and remediate a decidedly extractivist space into a meeting place where anti-colonial practices of visiting can be opened and followed.

We view L'Hirondelle as an *expert tracker*, an individual who charts new pathways of discovery that extends this knowledge as a gift to others. L'Hirondelle has learned from her years spent in communication with incarcerated artistic collaborators about the pathways and tactics of circumventing disciplinary enclosures. In keeping with her principle of radical inclusivity, the collaboratively produced tracks she lays are open for others to follow. In short, L'Hirondelle's art reveals welcoming pathways of visiting within the context of incarceration for Indigenous peoples and settlers alike. Moreover, in documenting her journey and story, L'Hirondelle's practice of tracking is developed with an invitation for others to echo her method, which begins to imagine and build something enduring – an infrastructure that extends from the provisional tracks of the media scarce.

Following the tracks of the caged bird

The healers have come, my spirit is free
The women are singing, bless my mouth
("Here I Am (Bless My Mouth)" 2013)

L'Hirondelle's *Why the Caged Bird Sings* imagines an anti-colonial track of resistance, one that helps us step outside the limits of carceral media scarcity towards a progressive decarceration agenda. To realize the process of decarceration, extensive work and care are needed: networks of connection must be maintained across media "divides" to ensure that the possibilities for public recognition of the struggles of the media scarce are expanded and in so doing collectively realize pathways of change. L'Hirdonelle's artistic collaboration responds to this challenge by demonstrating how the boundary of a digital divide can be transformed into a track, primed for the laying and layering of a subversive political infrastructure – what we are calling a *ceremonial infrastructure*. Specifically, L'Hirondelle's multimedia work remediates the disciplinary infrastructure of prison visitation, prison libraries, various entertainment media, payphones, and social media into a track of Indigenous ceremony and wayfinding. As Canadian scholars (and in Stephen's case, a Métis scholar), we choose this work not only for its remarkable artistic merit but also for the transformative potential of its mobilization of nêhiyawin with regard to conditions of incarceration.

Why the Caged Bird Sings circumvents conditions of carceral media scarcity to ensure that the project's songs and stories have a pathway to resonate with audiences who may otherwise feel "divided" by such struggles. Upon hearing the lyrics and emotive power of the music, it is impossible to miss the personal significance that these songs must have for the incarcerated collaborators as they deal so forcefully with issues of pain, loss, hope, and survival. This personal dimension is essential to the ceremonial function of the project, yet it is through L'Hirondelle's guiding of a communication network that the divide of media scarcity becomes remediated and that a public is invited to further imagine an anti-colonial track of carceral reform.

The seeds of inspiration for L'Hirondelle's work and its ceremonial infrastructure were planted in 1998 when she was invited to perform a musical concert at the Pine Groves Female Correctional Centre in Saskatchewan (L'Hirondelle 2015, 6).[2] According to L'Hirondelle, the concert became a pivotal moment for her when she was asked by an inmate to sing the "The Strong Woman Song". As part of custom, L'Hirondelle shared with the women how and from whom she learned the story of the song and its message: In the 1980s at the Kingston Prison for Women, a riot broke out and triggered a prison lockdown. Worried about this, a group of women began singing and drumming to "Maggie Paul's round dance song", and, as the story goes, all those who sang were not disrupted by the guards during the lockdown, and none of their eyes were affected by the guards' pepper spray. From that moment on, the song has been more commonly known as "The Strong Woman Song". From this event, L'Hirondelle became inspired to pursue her long-term songwriting project since, as she explains:

> I realised that by speaking of and telling the story of '*the Strong Woman Song*' – which is an uplifting recounting of an overcoming of adversity – I was given the honour of telling a bit of a local history not necessarily my own.
>
> (9)

Afterwards, not only were the women present in the room unified in the act of singing, but a sisterhood was also formed with the women in the story.

In a time of truth and reconciliation in Canada, this need for ceremony amongst Indigenous populations is particularly acute as pain and intergenerational trauma stemming from the history and ongoing legacy of Canadian colonialism is further unearthed, exposed, and painfully revisited. For instance, 2021 saw the locating of 215 unmarked graves of Indigenous children around the former Kamloops Indian Residential School, confirming the longstanding convictions of Indigenous nations, communities, and allies about the genocidal basis of the residential school system. Similarly, the ongoing crisis concerning missing and murdered Indigenous women and girls raises heartbreaking challenges and questions about the pathways for healing for families and communities. For those locked behind bars, ceremony in relation to these issues is sorely needed.

In this context, L'Hirondelle's practice of visiting seeks to help bring collaborators to heal together within an "emergent type of ceremonial society" (L'Hirondelle 2015, 54). It comes as no surprise that themes of colonial trauma, abuse, death, and grief arise so forcefully in the lyrics throughout *Why the Caged Bird Sings*:

> *I was someone's daughter in my younger years*   *Come my sisters, come*
> *The thunder is over, I'll cry no more tears*   *Come my sisters, come*
> *I wanna call a meeting and find our lost women*   *Come my sisters, come*
> *We've heard the ghost speak:*   *Come my sisters, come*
>   *'though dead I'm still living'*
>
> ("Come My Sisters, Come" 2011)

L'Hirondelle's practice of visiting and recording helps to construct a ceremonial society better able to occupy and retrack an oppressive colonizing infrastructure of prison media. Yet the political scope of L'Hirondelle's project is not limited to the physical visits of the songwriting and recording workshops, but it also extends to mediated forms of correspondence. L'Hirondelle provides all of her co-writers with her contact information and advises them to call her "collect". As a result, over the course of years, L'Hirondelle has been vetted by many prison case workers and added to several inmates' phone lists. In Canada, contact names for incarcerated people's phone list must first be approved by correctional services staff ("Inmate phone calls" 2019). Moreover, even in cases where contact with incarcerated women has been lost, L'Hirondelle (2015) reflects: "I find myself constantly trolling Facebook and other social media to find others – so that I can send them what is theirs – the finished, mastered recordings, along with any residual monies earned" (64). The delivery of the completed music is, in other words, central to the ceremonial function of L'Hirondelle's infrastructure, supported by record label Miyohtakwan Music. Through these means, L'Hirondelle maintains a network of tracking, care, and reciprocation.

Why the Caged Bird Sings was envisioned as an album, yet as of early 2023 it remains an incomplete collection of eight online songs ("Cheryl L'Hirondelle and friends" n.d.). One absent track from the collection is "Here I Am (Bless My Mouth)" (2013), a song co-written with incarcerated women and their literacy teacher at Okimaw Ohci Healing Lodge, a minimum-security federal prison located at Nekaneet First Nation in southwestern Saskatchewan. This absence is explained by L'Hirondelle's struggle with the conditions of media scarcity at the healing lodge as she was denied access by the warden to bring in any sound recording equipment for the sessions.

In response, L'Hirondelle developed a resourceful yet painstaking workaround: following the songwriting sessions, she remotely recorded the instrumentation and "scratch" demo vocals for the track, burned it onto a CD, and then sought clearance from the prison librarian to have it available for checkout. Collaborators in the session would then use their library card to sign out a CD player and CD to rehearse their vocals while listening to the song in preparation for a remote recording session over the phone. L'Hirondelle then sought formal inclusion on her collaborators' phone lists so that she would be able to correspond with each collaborator over time. This process accommodated her initial plan to have each woman sing their vocals over the telephone while listening to the track on the CD headphone. From this, L'Hirondelle would then record the co-writer's vocals over the phone. Ultimately, many of the collaborators were unable to borrow the CD and CD player from the library. What's more, L'Hirondelle was barred from many of their phone lists due to supposed security concerns, following intensive scrutiny and suspicion from prison staff.

During this process, unfortunately L'Hirondelle lost contact with many of her collaborators after some women were released or transferred to other facilities. Years later, still seeking to rectify the scarcity of voices on this record, L'Hirondelle has tracked down many of her collaborators on Facebook. The process has not been easy considering the lack of online documentation that many of her collaborators possess following their release from incarceration, which in some cases presumably stems from personal identity concerns or an ongoing lack of access to media. However, L'Hirondelle continues searching online for these women in the hopes of eventually recording and delivering a final version of the song and full album.

The ongoing recording work for "Here I Am (Bless My Mouth)" proceeds to this day, as L'Hirondelle seeks to finalize copyright agreements and acquire financial details from each of her collaborators so that publication earnings from the recording and any performances of the music can be appropriately distributed from an Escrow fund. The process of documentation for the sake of attribution and remuneration is integral to L'Hirondelle's politics of tracking as she seeks to correct the historical power imbalance perpetuated by the erasure of the identities of prison and chain gang song composers and performers. Following a review of prison and chain gang song recordings as collected by archivists such as Alan Lomax Jr., she comments:

> … As I delved more and more into these songs, in nearly every case, it was only possible to identify them [the composers and singers] by the names of the archivists who traveled around and collected them, or by the names of popular, folk and blues singers who had re-recorded them. In other words, the original singers and composers were not documented: their part in originating the work was largely invisible.
>
> (2015, 22)

L'Hirondelle's model of collective ownership of the work's copyright forcefully challenges the archivist's logic of sonic capture by countering the oppressive tendencies articulated by practices of "hungry listening", a Western mode of listening that is inextricably rooted in colonial logics of extraction and appropriative consumption (Robinson 2020). Notably, archival practices of documentation and attribution – or lack thereof – concerning prison and chain gang songs eerily echo the dual logic of extraction and deprivation that underpins the contemporary prison media complex and its form of surveillance capitalism by similarly alienating incarcerated people from the products of their media work: the recordist of chain gang songs is doubly hungry, so to speak, by extracting song and supplanting the identities of its creators for that of the field recorder himself.

In contrast, L'Hirondelle's nêhiyawin art practice embodies what Dylan Robinson (2020) calls "Indigenous ontologies of song" by inviting listeners to "reorient what we think we are listening to and how we go about our practices of listening with responsibilities to listen differently" (45). The collective ownership enacted through *Why the Caged Bird Sings* and the extensive work of tracking performed by L'Hirondelle realize this by helping audiences imagine a transformative pathway of documentation arising from conditions of media scarcity – one that would lead us outwards and beyond the confines of a Western colonial regime towards a re-emergent ceremonial society. This is perhaps best articulated, albeit tragically, with the case of Margaret Sewap who was murdered shortly following her release from Pine Grove correctional facility. In honour of her memory, L'Hirondelle sent a recording of Sewap's singing along with the lyrics she contributed on two songs for the project to her family. The artist reflects:

> Though the cause of her death was unrelated to the [songwriting] workshop, the artifact of her recorded voice and the legacy of her contribution to this canon of songs will surely be of consequence to her family and the community she leaves behind.

(2015, 63)

Evidently, the Indigenous sisterhood that L'Hirondelle brings forward manifests a remarkable healing power that retracks the carceral scarcity of documentation through song: in this case, by providing Sewap's family and loved ones with a trace of her spirit and creative spark – one that they might follow and retrace in their personal journey of healing.

Crossing a sonorous bridge

Part of L'Hirondelle's response to the pressures of carceral media scarcity on her own songwriting sessions for "Here I Am (Bless My Mouth)" was further developed during an artist residency entitled, "Reconsidering Reconciliation" (2013), at Thompson Rivers University in Kamloops located on Traditional Secwepemc Territories. For her contribution L'Hirondelle developed a remarkable re-staging of her collaborative journey through prison walls: her work functions as a kind of proxy art illustrating how media scarcity often involves unreliable and intermittent modes of communication restricted by surveillance and disciplinary management. Because L'Hirondelle was unable to record the songwriters' voices from Okimaw Ohci Healing Lodge, she decided to retrack this absence as a medium of collaborative witnessing whereby women at the residency were invited to sit in and sing on behalf of the women who had written "Here I Am (Bless My Mouth)".

At the residency, L'Hirondelle brought together a group of women artists and intellectuals to create videos and sound recordings of the incomplete song. For the production, each woman used a payphone and dialed a number to reach one of the other women participants to then sing the song in full. Each woman individually performed by singing along to a mock-up studio version of the song from which only the sonic output from the telephone receiver was recorded along with visual footage. This created an asynchronous event from which all of the voices were not brought together until much later in a subsequent installation exhibit that we discuss below.

In the residency, a powerful telephonic resonance is articulated as the stand-in women travelled to a semi-public location to use a payphone at the cafeteria of Thompson Rivers University. Further, the modulated sound quality of singing voices over the telephone receiver echoes the impoverished state of mediated communication within prison, while the blurred-out video image of the women's faces bears an arresting resemblance to publicly re-posted CCTV footage – distantly resonating with the conditions of surveillance and institutional oversight of the prison (see Figure 3.1).

Ayumi Goto, one of the invited stand-ins at L'Hirondelle's residency, characterized her experience of the piece as one of participation in a kind of "sonorous bridge" (2018, 150), an unlikely first meeting place between seemingly disparate lives through song. In deep reflection, she wrote:

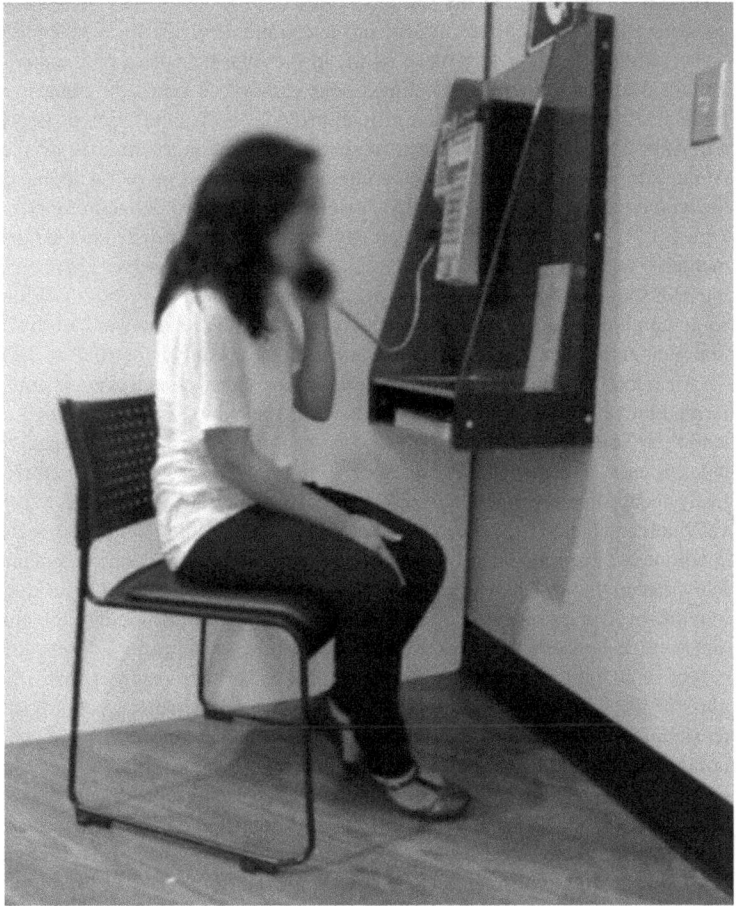

Figure 3.1 A collaborator standing in for an absent voice on "Here I Am (Bless My Mouth)".

38 Retracking incarceration

> The echoing of actions of sitting in front of the payphone, making a call, singing into the receiver, and then listening in to the voice of another, created an embodied affiliation between the women incarcerated and the women at the artist residency.
>
> (150)

This telephonic resonance thus further extends the ceremonial infrastructure of the project well beyond the carceral conditions of media scarcity by incorporating new voices and listeners within the meeting place of song.

Tracking this further into a series of exhibits held between 2013 and 2020,[3] L'Hirondelle has featured the residency project as a multimedia installation consisting of a series of ten tablets and telephone receivers fixed to gallery walls. Without seeking to replace or fill in the missing voices of the songwriters from Okimaw Ohci Healing Lodge, this piece keeps the song in a fragmented and digitally grainy form yet provides a medium through which a transformative act of visiting can follow – an invitation to cross the divide. At the exhibits, each tablet offers a unique point of contact or visit with one of the women who have stood in for the original incarcerated collaborators (see Figure 3.2). Visitors to the exhibits are invited to listen and relisten to the fragmented song from the position of multiple women, who themselves are operating as a sonorous bridge to the voices of the incarcerated songwriters. While some iterations of the exhibit do not include chairs, the refrain and call to action remain the same: visit and sit or stand with these women (see Figure 3.3).

An embodied practice of telephonic visiting – of answering a call – is transformed into a resonant practice of solidarity as the exhibit visitor is invited to lend their voice and sing along. And so, a second, unsounded call is made to break silence, to remediate any distance with the media scarce, and to collectively occupy its track of resistance. What is perhaps typically imagined as a "private" call conducted between incarcerated subject and visitor – tarnished by the conditions of institutional surveillance and crowded visitation rooms – remains individuated for the listener, and yet, the invitation to sing along and speak out into the receiver envelops the gallery into a public space of action through mediated extensions of L'Hirondelle's ceremonial infrastructure.

By remediating the plexi-glass partition of a prison visitation with the glass of the tablet and telephone receiver, the work navigates a paradoxical tension, feeling both close and distant, immediate and mediated, personal and unfamiliar, simultaneously intimate and institutional. From this unlikely site of visiting, what trace of the call remains for the visitor who freely returns home after replacing the receiver and leaving the gallery? Like the chorus of the songbird, "both question and answer and ever-repeating" (L'Hirondelle 2014, 161): Might the song become quietly lodged in the back of the throat, waiting to be resounded and retracked?

Retracking incarceration 39

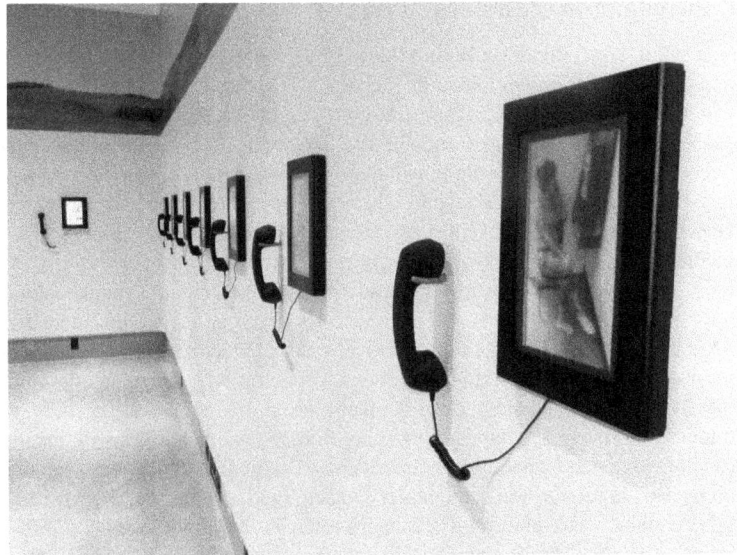

Figure 3.2 "Here I am (Bless My Mouth)" exhibit.

Figure 3.3 "Here I am (Bless My Mouth)" exhibit with chairs.

Concluding: an open track

The "Here I am (Bless My Mouth)" series of exhibits helps to reimagine how audience distance and divides with media scarce individuals and communities can be remade into a space of amplification, resonance, and commiseration – a shared space between L'Hirondelle and her incarcerated collaborators, between the women proxies digitally lodged within the tablets, amongst the gallery visitors and audiences beyond. The work remediates a felt divide between singer and listener and unsettles any boundary between the media scarce and media abundant, effectively retracing this as a track that others can follow, extend, and occupy. Notably, this does not strive to "give voice to the voiceless" but imparts a call to amplify and occupy a seat of resonance within a network. Moreover, we suggest that the call to visit with and listen to these women does more than allow incarcerated voices and a specific lyrical message to cross the divide; rather, the message of the work lies in the method and medium of tracking itself, one that deviates with care from the pathways of institutionally sanctioned prison visitation and instead allows audiences to hear these women on terms that are far less dehumanized, disciplined, and remote. Specifically, L'Hirondelle's ceremonial infrastructure retracks the divide of prison media as an open track – no longer as a boundary or enclosure. She writes (2014, 151–152):

> …To many Native people a "divide" also refers to the beautiful vistas and intricate landscapes of the geological term that connotes watersheds, ridges of land between two drainage basins and/or that of the grandiosity of a continental divide…For Native people, a divide therefore is not a binary, an either/or – it is rich with variety and the means of our sustenance and continued survival.

The track is already in place, and it can always be returned to – it is home, and it is the land. This is beautifully expressed in the visual backdrop for the "Here I Am (Bless My Mouth)" exhibits in an expansive panorama photograph of rural Saskatchewan, spanning across the room above the tablets and phone receivers reminding gallery visitors that prison cannot hold these women and their songs. No, as the artist says, because only Mother Earth can hold them.[4] Through song, L'Hirondelle transforms the bounded space of incarceration – its walls, its punitive structure and media logic – into a chorus that echoes and signposts but also opens and extends, as onto a lyrical verse or musical bridge.

Thus, the aesthetic work of tracking not only remediates what is designed to divide and conquer or what is meant to silence, but it also seeks to guide others forward through questions, answers, and songbird calls. And yet, crucially, although gallery visitors are invited to visit through L'Hirondelle's infrastructure and are even called upon to sing, sit, and stand with the incarcerated songwriters, the song does not need their recognition to become heard. The ceremonial infrastructure will continue to resonate for L'Hirondelle's collaborators as their songs lead them forward and help them find their way home. Again, quoting the song in refrain:

> *The healers have come, my spirit is free*
> *The women are singing, bless my mouth.*
> ("Here I Am (Bless My Mouth)" 2013)

It is not the visitor's blessing as a listener that is addressed within the lyrics but a blessing that occupies the track of the ceremonial society. Thus, as listeners we are simply invited to take up the caged bird's song and follow it so as to break the silent or unspoken privilege that comes within a culture of media abundance. Perhaps then the perceived divide between the incarcerated and the free might be experienced more as an opening and meeting place whereupon the challenging work of reimagining incarceration can be nourished.

Finally, perhaps then the unfinished track of "Here I Am (Bless My Mouth)" as a deliverable sound recording has led L'Hirondelle – the expert tracker – onto something more expansive and enduring that will continue to guide others to follow and push onward. Through her navigation of the barriers of prison media, she has not only documented a repertoire of tactics that lead from conditions of media scarcity but left behind signposts for a counter political infrastructure – an amplifying and resonant network. A series of provisional tracks (e.g. the demo version, the scratch vocals, and the installation) currently embody "Here I Am (Bless My Mouth)", yet it is through L'Hirondelle's reiterative work of retracking that an infrastructural appropriation of prison media takes shape. Let us see and listen where this leads, but let us not remain detached from its songbird calls.

Notes

1 Historically, the term "halfbreed" was often used derogatorily to refer to individuals with mixed European and Indigenous ancestry. However, many Métis people reappropriate this term to valorize their distinct cultural identity (see Campbell 1973). Following Campbell, L'Hirondelle (2015, 1) explains that she introduces herself as a Halfbreed to express that Métis own themselves (*ka-atapimisohcik*). L'Hirondelle has kinship with many card-carrying members of various Alberta Metis Nation locals yet identifies as Halfbreed herself. She explains further that following many conversations and teachings offered from Maria Cambell regarding the complexity of Indigenous identity that she prefers to honour how differently she feels about her identity "instead of merely ascribing to the shorthand self naming that Metis or First Nations has become" (personal correspondence).
2 In Canada, like other colonial nation states, Indigenous people are alarmingly overrepresented in prisons: Indigenous adults account for roughly 28 percent of admissions to provincial, territorial, and federal prisons yet only constitute about 5 percent of the adult population in Canada (Maleakieh 2018). This gross overrepresentation

42 *Retracking incarceration*

is even more apparent for Indigenous women who make up 43 percent of female admissions to provincial prisons, and about half of all federally sentenced women (Jacobs 2022; Maleakieh 2018).
3 https://algomaufineartandmusic.wordpress.com/2014/03/09/cheryl-lhirondelle-at-the-art-gallery-of-algoma/; https://theimagecentre.ca/exhibition/ghost-dance-activism-resistance-art/; https://paherald.sk.ca/new-art-exhibit-allows-public-to-engage-with-songs-written-by-inmates/.
4 From personal correspondence with L'Hirondelle.

Bibliography

Arguelles, Paolo, and Isabelle Ortiz-Luis. 2021. "Bars Behind Bars: Digital Technology in the Prison System." SSRN Scholarly Paper. Rochester, NY. https://doi.org/10.2139/ssrn.3812046.

Campbell, Maria. 1973. *Halfbreed*. Toronto: McClelland and Stewart.

Certeau, Michel de. 1984. *The Practice of Everyday Life*. Translated by Steven Randall. Berkeley: University of California Press.

"Cheryl L'Hirondelle and Friends." n.d. bandcamp. Accessed October 19, 2023. https://whythecagedbirdsings.bandcamp.com.

"Come My Sisters, Come". 2011. SOCAN/Miyohtakwan Music. Written & recorded October 3–7, Pine Grove Correctional Centre, Prince Albert, SK. Lyrics by: Maureen Montgrand, Elizabeth "Lizzie" Charles, Bernice Bighead, Deanna Renee Desjarlais, Melody Bird, Angela Rabbitskin, M. Henderson, Carla Johnson-Powell. Music by: C. L'Hirondelle and G. Hoskins. Performed by: vocals – Maureen Montrand, Elizabeth Charles, Bernice Sanderson, Deanna Renee Desjarlais, Melody Bird, Angela Rabbitskin, M. Henderson, Carla Johnson-Powell, Cheryl L'Hirondelle; spoken word – Bernice Sanderson; percussion – Cheryl L'Hirondelle; guitars and drum programming – Gregory Hoskins; bass – Colleen Hodgson. Recorded by: Gregory Hoskins, Additional recording, instrumentation, mixed and mastered by: David Travers.

Farley, Helen. 2018. "Using 3D Worlds in Prison: Driving, Learning and Escape." *Journal of Virtual Worlds Research* 11 (1): 1–11. https://doi.org/10.4101/jvwr.v11i1.7304.

Goto, Ayumi. 2018. "共同生活 (Kyōdōseikatsu): In the Shadows of Witnessing." Simon Fraser University. https://summit.sfu.ca/item/18620.

"Here I Am (Bless My Mouth)". 2013. SOCAN/Miyohtakwan Music. Written April 15–19, Okimaw Ohci Healing Lodge, Nekaneet First Nation, SK. Lyrics by Catherine McAlinden, Christine Griffiths, Heike Irmgard Hagen, Sherry Wright, Beverly Fullerton, RM Gorman, Lori ann Maurice, Kristen Dillon, Katie Brunet, Tiffany Peters, E. Jackman, Panda Bear Delorme, Vonetta Martin, Cyndi Sinclair. Music by: C. L'Hirondelle and G. Hoskins. Unpublished recording.

"Inmate Phone Calls." 2019. Government website. Correctional Service Canada. January 17, 2019. https://www.csc-scc.gc.ca/family/003004-0004-en.shtml.

Jacobs. 2022. "Half of the Women in Canada's Federal Prisons Are Indigenous." *NPR*. May 10, 2022. https://www.npr.org/2022/05/10/1098014745/nearly-half-the-women-in-canadas-federal-prisons-are-indigenous#:~:text=JACOBS%3A%20Less%20than%205%25%20of,Canada's%20correctional%20investigator%20Ivan%20Zinger.

Jewkes, Yvonne, and Helen Johnston. 2009. "'Cavemen in an Era of Speed-of-Light Technology': Historical and Contemporary Perspectives on Communication within Prisons." *The Howard Journal of Criminal Justice* 48 (2): 132–143. https://doi.org/10.1111/j.1468-2311.2009.00559.x.

Jewkes, Yvonne, and Bianca C. Reisdorf. 2016. "A Brave New World: The Problems and Opportunities Presented by New Media Technologies in Prisons." *Criminology & Criminal Justice* 16 (5): 534–551. https://doi.org/10.1177/1748895816654953.

Kaun, Anne, and Fredrik Stiernstedt. 2022. "Prison Tech: Imagining the Prison as Lagging Behind and as a Test Bed for Technology Advancement." *Communication, Culture and Critique* 15 (1): 69–83. https://doi.org/10.1093/ccc/tcab032.

Kaun, Anne, and Fredrik Stiernstedt. 2023. *Prison Media: Incarceration and the Infrastructures of Work and Technology*. Cambridge, MA: MIT Press.

Kisynska, Sylwia. 2016. "The Elders Say We Don't Visit Anymore." *Gallery Gachet* (blog). 2016. http://gachet.org/2016/06/07/the-elders-say-we-dont-visit-anymore/.

L'Hirondelle, Cheryl. 2014. "Codetalkers Recounting Signals of Survival." In *Coded Territories: Tracing Indigenous Pathways in New Media Art*, edited by Steven Loft and Kerry Swanson, 1st edition, 41–168. Calgary, Alberta, Canada: University of Calgary Press.

L'Hirondelle, Cheryl. 2015. "Why the Caged Bird Sings: Radical Inclusivity, Sonic Survivance and the Collective Ownership of Freedom Songs." Masters, OCAD University. https://openresearch.ocadu.ca/id/eprint/287/.

Maleakieh, Jamil. 2018. "Adult and Youth Correctional Statistics in Canada, 2017/2018." *Statistics Canada*. https://www150.statcan.gc.ca/n1/pub/85-002-x/2019001/article/00010-eng.htm.

Robinson, Dylan. 2020. *Hungry Listening: Resonant Theory for Indigenous Sound Studies*. Minneapolis: University of Minnesota Press.

Tetrault, Justin E. C. 2022. "Indigenizing Prisons: A Canadian Case Study." *Crime and Justice* 51, 187–236. https://doi.org/10.1086/720943.

Van de Steene, Steven, and Victoria Knight. 2017. "Digitizing the Prison: The Light and Dark Future." *Prison Service Journal* 231: 22–30.

4 Re-staging the Soviet secret city
The good life, the toxic life

If you searched Google image for "secret cities", what might you expect to find? Maybe nothing; they are "secret" after all. Or maybe they are no longer secret, and evidence has since surfaced, circulating freely amidst the abundance of information online. Over 30 years after the end of the cold war, you might expect to see declassified glimpses of life from what used to be tightly restricted, so-called secret cities. The media documentation of life in secret cities in the former Soviet Union was, however, strictly curtailed and regulated, resulting in a scarcity of information about these places that persists to this day. Many contemporary secret cities remain media scarce. It should come as no surprise then that Google searches for "Soviet secret cities" typically return little beside aerial photos, sanitized in their remoteness, of generic urban landscape. There are few street-level images that tell of work, culture, leisure, or everyday life.

However, secret cities were not – and are not – moribund or redundant, either in the lasting memories of its inhabitants or as refashioned by post-Soviet economic and security policies. Common images of secret cities do not fully represent daily life as experienced by its citizens. Moreover, as we shall see in this chapter, while secret cities were media scarce places in Soviet times, their continued remediation as bombed out, post-human spaces obscures more than it reveals of their past, present, and future.

Secret cities are also referred to as "closed cities", and often "Soviet secret cities", given the eastward glance of much of the scholarly literature, contemporary Western geopolitical anxieties, and photographic lenses. Putin's invasion of Ukraine has likely only amplified this perspective. Kate Brown's (2013) comparative study of US and Russian "atomic cities" follows this trajectory, as does urbanist Keller Easterling's (2014) analysis of the "Russian Science City" in her popular book *Extrastatecraft: The Power of Infrastructure Space*. In both books, two aspects of closed, secret cities are central. The first is the recognition of a city that is distinct from others, almost universally secluded from the rest of the nation and world surrounded by walls, fences, and checkpoints that strictly control entry and exit. Secret cities are often purposefully excluded from maps; they are surreptitiously built and maintained, to be revealed to the world some day.

There was also a common ideological sense of purpose in secret cities, given their importance for scientific and security interests, and the corresponding cultivation of a privileged "class-less" society within its perimeters. Secret cities were relatively wealthy cities, with enviable educational, leisure, and health infrastructure. Thus, secure border crossings also literally and figuratively separated residents from the grim economic reality of life in much of the USSR. As a consequence, citizens of secret cities largely supported the security measures – including the restrictions on taking photos and videos of city life – that produced a media scarce "picture" of these towns and homes. In other words, the authoritarian life of media scarcity was largely embraced, as Kate Brown notes in her book entitled *Plutopia*. In both the Soviet Union and the United States, Brown argues that life in the secret city was regarded fondly by its residents:

> [Nuclear Cities]… generated happy childhood memories, affordable housing, and excellent schools in prize-winning model communities that became havens for the new nuclear families that inhabited them. The plutonium pioneers…. recall never having to lock their doors, children roaming safely, friendly neighbours, and the absence of unemployment, indigence, and crime.
>
> (3)

Apart from seclusion, economic security, and secrecy, the other main characteristic of such cities is a strict focus on economy – on opaque business, industry, and work. Margit Zuckriel confirms this thesis: "Closed Cities are… communities defined and created for a particular purpose, architectural and urban surrogates pragmatically designed to accommodate work forces or to allow some particular work to be performed" (249). Zuckriel, however, curiously contends that closed cities have not evolved over time.

Not surprisingly, representations of the closed city in books, popular essays, and documentary films largely focus on their nuclear, military arms, mining, and other secretive research activities (Goetschel 2005, 2016). These were largely "company towns", not unlike the Western industrial cities that thrived in the 1950s – think iron production companies in cities throughout the Ohio River valley, the pulp and paper mills along the west coast of Canada, or the coal mines in the valleys of southern Wales. And just as many of these one industry towns started to suffer and collapse in the 1970s, so too did many closed, secret, or nuclear cities after the collapse of the Soviet Union, especially after the successful negotiation of arms treaties.

In part, given the historical dynamics at play in secret cities, we disagree with Zuckriel that secret cities do not "evolve". Rather, by contrasting the photographic projects of two artists and, to a lesser extent, a documentary film-maker, this chapter argues that media scarce secret cities should not be interpreted as empty, lacking in historical change, or political contestation. We begin with Gregor Sailer's (2012) *Closed Cities* collection of photographs that offer an unrelenting image of the modern-day secret city – one of decay, brought on by decades of isolation, geographic marginalization, anonymity, and secrecy. Sailer's professional photography portfolio offers a consistent sensibility, aesthetic, and subject matter – windswept landscapes, concrete infrastructures, and industrial blight (Sailer n.d.). In his most recent exhibition, a retrospective of his work entitled "Unseen Places", Sailer (2022) compliments themes exposed in *Closed Cities* with images of "…surreal architectures at the margins of human civilization…Inaccessible landscapes, sealed-off territories and restricted military areas". Verena Kaspar-Eisert (2023) thus categorizes Sailer's art as a form of "New Objectivity" "…characterized by his quiet, unpretentious, and serious artistic approach, which also manifests formally in his photographs: he attempts, with his pictures, to lend structure to a confusing world" (10–11).

By comparison, in Sergey Novikov's (2019a) collaboratively produced photography book entitled *ZATO* (the post-cold war term for a Russian tax-free zone), the secret city is retrospectively depicted as having offered a relatively privileged life, yet one that was also toxic, both environmentally and socially. *ZATO* performs such contradictions from the media scarce city, over 30 years after the fall of the Soviet Union. The staging of its photographs memorializes life in the media scarce city, while at the same time reflecting upon its newfound political, economic, and environmental toxicity.

Unlike Sailer, Novikov's photographic art is decidedly playful and ironic, masking a subtle political critique. Novikov's *ZATO* represents an effort at documenting a media scarce history of such secret places, not just as unknown cities but as lived experiences. The campy and otherwise absurd staged poses of former residents often highlight the social and environmental costs of the secret city. Novikov's photographic subjects and spaces often blur fact and fiction as a means of mediating history and politics. For example, in his project entitled "Closer than Switzerland", Novikov (2019b) captured an "Imaginative series [of images] that addresses the issue of the impact of troubled banks on the economy and culture of Latvia". Like Novikov's other projects, including *ZATO*, photos depict a wide range of human activities, objects, and architectures that call into question the dubious role that Latvia's banking system plays in mediating corrupt economic relations between the east and the west.

The uninhabited secret city?

At first glance, the opening spread in Sailer's *Closed Cities* is rather stark. It starts with a decidedly barren map. Closed cities are represented by six small

Restaging the Soviet secret city 47

Figure 4.1 Clothes drying in the wind. Photograph courtesy of Gregor Sailer.

dots, accompanied by names, country or state abbreviations: Nordelta (AR), Mirny (RUS), and so on. The map, spanning both pages, is encircled by longitude and latitude degrees, east, west, north, and south. At the bottom right, a small scale in miles and kilometres. This is scarce cartography.

The sparse nature of this "table of contents-as-map" not so subtly sets the stage for Sailer's subsequent series of photos. These are more than isolated locations. They are unrepresented on common maps. The cities are largely unknown, or at the very least under-documented. There is an ecological and environmental consistency to Sailer's photographs: they depict barren, depressing, and inhospitable spaces, cities, and landscapes. A particularly stark series of photos represent domestic architectures from brutalist Soviet apartment blocks. Throughout the book, humans are entirely absent, silencing the voices of former media scarce residents.

In the afterword of *Closed Cities*, Margit Zuckriegel's refers to the collection of photos as depicting a "no-mans land" or simply as "neutral" (251). On the surface, these spaces, sites, and architectures are seemingly unfit for human life, let alone happiness. Yet if we look closely, that's not entirely so. Traces of human life persist in many photos, for example, through an image capturing clothes drying in the wind (see Figure 4.1), provoking questions. Are these ecological wastelands? Have they been abandoned or ravaged by war? Where are the inhabitants? Have they fled? Clearly, they have not since a select number of Sailer's images depict economic activity – exhaust or steam billows from a chimney in one photo, illuminated lights, and street lamps are seen in others, while dust emanates from a deep and wide mining pit in one particularly grandiose two-page photo. (see Figure 4.2).

Figure 4.2 Dust emanates from a deep and wide mining pit. Photograph courtesy of Gregor Sailer.

Sailer's *Closed City* collection of photographs, while captured between 2010 and 2011, clearly invoke a longer historical narrative. Yet the photos seemingly freeze time, in part because there is no human movement, here are only imagined bodies, workers, and residents. But who are these people? The cities appear to have been abandoned, the secret city residents replaced by pollution, dust, and clouds of particles that suggest an extraction-heavy economy. These closed cities are digging, burning fossil fuels: isn't there an impact on humans? Is there a human story among this media scarcity?

ZATO: from fusion to tax credits

Just like many cities and urban zones around the world, Russian secret cities rebranded themselves as forward-looking centres of economic production during the *perestroika* (or economic reform) years following the fall of the Soviet Union (1991-onwards). In 1995, for example, Russian government officials held what *The Times* reported was "an extraordinary trade exhibition in Moscow" highlighting the economic shift in closed, secret cities from "swords to sofas" and other domestic products. According to the report, "The competition among the secret cities is stiff" (Beeston 1995). Three short years later, Russian secret cities witnessed another attempt at rebranding their closed image. In 1998, a number of secret cities working in conjunction with American state and industry officials "launched an ambitious scheme ...to turn Russia's 12 secret cities – homes of its top nuclear scientists and technicians – into silicon valleys". Former US Energy Secretary Bill Richardson exclaimed that "We are putting $30 million of US taxpayers' money into helping people start small businesses. I am confident US businesses will follow" (Masterman 1998).

Following Margaret Thatcher's early 1980s experiment with "enterprise" or tax-free zones (Thornley 1991) and other financial inducements for businesses to move into economically deprived areas, post-Soviet secret cities became exceptional jurisdictions designed to foster neoliberal forms of financial experimentation, though economic analyses suggested that they were highly dependent on the Russian federal budget in the 1990s (Brock 1998, 1078). Other myths of private wealth were also called into question. As a new Russian secret city emerged in the 1990s, the myth of the classless 1950s secret city – the *plutopia* – was replaced by the 1990s business models of fossil fuel extraction and tax avoidance. Hence, it might be more appropriate to say that such cities were not so much exceptional, as *integral* in the financial sense of the world, offering spaces from which the booming Russian oil and gas industries could escape taxation and other forms of oversight and regulation.

Part of the rebranding and restructuring of secret city economies included renaming the city space itself. In 1992, mirroring efforts to liberalize the Russian economy for foreign investment and divest itself of some nuclear armaments and associated industries, secret cities were renamed "closed administrative territorial formations" (*Zakrytye Administrativno-Territorial'nye Obrazovaniya*), or simply "ZATO". According to Sixsmith (2010), the Russian government introduced new laws that

> Gave ZATOs the right to "grant additional reductions in taxes and fees to legal entities that are registered as taxpayers…Firms operating there were allowed to enjoy the same beneficial tax status traditionally associated with offshore havens such as the Bahamas or the British Channel Islands."
> (192)

"Fuel producers had to pay excise. For optimising this tax, the factory capacity of refineries was rented to companies registered in ZATO" (Glazunov 2016,164). Not surprisingly, oil and gas companies flooded into ZATO territories, often setting up shell offices that brought few jobs.[1] Russian government investigators determined "that 'hundreds of millions of dollars in taxes' were under-collected from firms using ZATOS, including many oil companies" (Sixsmith 2010, 192).

As ZATO cities continue to secure their borders to varying degrees, foreign visits continue to be highly regulated and media restricted. After many financial projects from the 1990s failed, mining and weaponry have re-emerged as core secretive economies. Moreover, as Russia began a slow turn under Putin to a more authoritarian domestic politics, chipping away at opposition voices, civil society organizations, and alternative media opinions, the toxicity of the secret cities – as with many of the gulags that predated such economies[2] – has begun to reveal itself.

Inhabiting ZATO

If Gregor Sailer's *Closed Cities* photo essay served to establish inhuman economies at the center of the secret city, Sergey Novikov's (2019a) photo essay book aptly entitled *ZATO* offers a contemporary, if not partially retrospective, reassessment of secret cities through the staged memories of its citizens and former inhabitants. His project, in other words, offers a compelling example of media scarce art and storytelling where former residents collaborate to represent the secret city life. The media scarce life is revisited, retold, and re-enacted by its residents.

Novikov's collection of photographs opens on a similar cartographic note to Sailer, though he anchors his imagery with text:

> These [secret] cities did not appear on any maps, had encrypted names and were called "mailboxes" – much like secret manufacturing facilities located within these cities that had no specific address, but rather a mailbox where all their post was sent. The inhabitants of these cities were instructed not to refer to their place of residence, but rather to use the name of the nearest major city…
>
> (1)

A closer link between the secret city and the body of its inhabitants is established in Novikov's photo of a mailbox hoisted in the air by a pair of arms (see Figure 4.3). We cannot see the subjects' face or even portion of their head, yet a series of numbers written on one outstretched arm foregrounds the book's biopolitical undertones.

Thus, while Sailer forces us to imagine the inhabitants and workers in secret economies and spaces, Novikov's secret citizens are omnipresent in the photographs, both as subjects of the camera lens and as performers, that is, as active recreators of former lives. These distinctions are further amplified by the differences in the production of the two books. *Closed Cities* assembles photographs captured by a visual artist, with a reputation built upon a series of books and multiple public gallery exhibitions. Sailer's book includes commentary and critiques from established art critics. *ZATO* is decidedly populist by contrast, built upon an internet-enabled collaboration among several current and former ZATO inhabitants. Novikov curates the media scarce "staged" photos or performances but does not capture them through his own lens. Novikov explains the book's modus operandi:

> Project ZATO is a visualization of the memories of residents of closed-cities and my own experience of visiting these places, inspired by discussions on web forums, announcements by municipal authorities, and publications on social media sites. The photographs are staged, and the project does not contain any photos that I took myself in the closed cities.
>
> (1)

Restaging the Soviet secret city 51

Figure 4.3 Mailbox hoisted in the air by a pair of arms. Photograph courtesy of Sergey Novikov.

While some photos re-stage specific moments and memories of secret city citizens, many ZATO photographs also retrospectively highlight the environmental and social costs of a seemingly protected and privileged life. Brown (2013) reminds us, through the image of a *Plutopia*, of the economic contradictions of the secret city. While offering riches and a lifestyle unparalleled for the working class and their families, the by-products of many secret city industries were hazardous to human life. Many images in ZATO highlight this glaring contradiction produced by the media scarce, secret city as a good yet toxic life.

The representation of such contradictions, as a critique of ZATO and Russian life, are subtly masked in ironic, humourous, and absurdly staged images. The more absurd the photo (e.g. pose of the collaborator), the more explicit the critique is of the toxic secret city. We might question though if many

52 *Restaging the Soviet secret city*

images even make sense to those outside of Russia or secret cities. Some images are in-jokes, and others decidedly campy representations of authoritarian life in the ZATO: a bare-chested man holds a glass to the wall to listen in on a neighbour (see Figure 4.4); a woman is handcuffed to a tree in a forest; a man with a red armband signals another man to stop; a long corrugated steel security fence goes for as far as the eye can see; and so on.

Conversely, there are also reminders of how the citizen subjects of the secret city embraced authoritarian surveillance and security, again as a "protected" life, though along decidedly toxic, often xenophobic, lines. Next to the image of the bare-chested surveillant neighbour, we see a large apartment complex. Novikov's accompanying text reminds us that there are no criminal elements in the secret city housing market (16). In another two-page photo, three secret city citizens converge on a street corner where a man of Asian

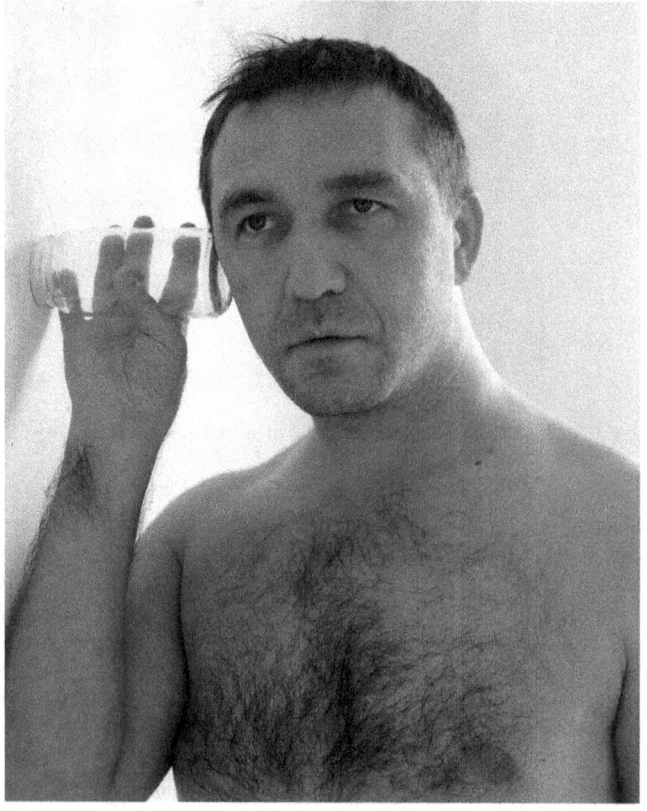

Figure 4.4 A bare-chested man holds a glass to the wall. Photograph courtesy of Sergey Novikov.

descent looks for directions on a handheld map. A mother stares at the stranger holding her child's hand firmly, while keeping her distance. Most striking though is ZATO's cover which depicts a man at a barbed wire fence. He holds a roll of wire in his hand, though it is unclear if he is adding to or removing the fence. The text above his head reads: "I wonder what kind of homosexuals could have voted to open up the town".

The toxicity of ZATO is also, as we have already seen, economic and environmental. Novikov's choice of photos is much less ambiguous or opaque on this point. Many of these photos focus on environmental toxins and nuclear waste, particularly in water. In one photo, a man taking a bath stares at a can of drinking water floating among the bubbles; in another, a hooded figure is seen fishing next to nuclear submarines in a harbour. The nuclear theme is repeated in a photograph of another bare-chested man up to his knees in a lake waving a flag with nuclear images. Vladmir Putin's iconic bare-chested "remasculinization of Russia" photograph is thus reframed, repositioned, isolated, and toxic (Riabov and Riabova 2014).

Brown (2013) argues that such toxic and environmental hazards of life in secret cities presented a trade-off of sorts, though it is arguable whether its citizens were fully aware of such dangers. She writes: "As Plutopia matured, residents gave up their civil *and biological rights* for consumer rights" (our emphasis). Brown's secret cities were utopian in many respects (middle-class lives for working-class workers), but their economic experiments with plutonium would have long-lasting health impacts on secret city residents (5). Brown, in other words, amplifies the secret city as a site of biopolitical experimentation.

As nuclear and other toxic industries closed or left, some secret cities moved on from financial experiments and tax havens to pharmaceutical and other life science-based economic models. Sarov, a former nuclear city, for example, partnered with several American health researchers in the late 1990s to study asthma. Indeed, from the outset, citizens in secret cities, particularly nuclear cities, were subject to intense "medical surveillance" (Brown 2013, 67). The secret city became a human laboratory for scientists studying the effects of radiation on the environment, the food supply, and humans. A parallel theme is captured in *ZATO*, where a photo depicts a young woman with green spots all over her face (see Figure 4.5). The photo on the facing page shows a set of red and yellow pills next to the accompanying text: "Triazavrin (TZV) is a broad-spectrum antiviral drug developed in the closed town of Novouralsk. Triazavrin is effective against 15 types of influenza… Triazavrin could save the world from Ebola fever".

Iconic secret cities

To suggest that the secret city is an uninhabited space, or worse a space devoid of history or human stories, would paper over a toxic biopolitical history. In *ZATO*, the media scarce history of secret cities is re-embodied, though not

Figure 4.5 A young woman with green spots all over her face. Photograph courtesy of Sergey Novikov.

only through photographed re-enactments of memories previously uncaptured by media but also by the knowledge of the toxicity of such spaces that emerged after the fall of the Soviet Union. As the name of the project itself suggests, Novikov's *ZATO* strategically uses media scarcity to highlight ZATO's toxic economy with the previous secret city's "comfortable" yet similarly toxic racism and xenophobia. Yet in Novikov's subsequent project, he takes media scarcity to another level, where the secret city remains restricted, yet iconic. Media is scarce, but what remains takes on an even greater importance, socially, politically, and culturally. The iconic images of the secret city are hard to ignore; their scarcity becomes an aesthetic dogma and, consequently for Novikov and his collaborators, a site of political contestation.

Following the *ZATO* secret city project, Novikov headed to a remote, closed Russian arctic city. While *ZATO* served to perform a media scarce past, Novikov uses the closed Arctic city of Norilsk to fictionalize and thus subvert iconic yet cliched images of the arctic city. Norilsk's iconic status derives from its history as a Soviet Gulag but also as the largest permafrost grounded city above the Arctic circle (Shiklomanov and Laruelle 2017, 253). While the city is restricted and regulated in much the same way as others depicted in *Closed Cities* and *ZATO*, it also serves as an iconic, universal sign, an all-encompassing image of the Soviet and later Russian Arctic. In Soviet times, Norilsk served as a symbol of Soviet mastery over the natural elements; for Putin, it provided a hub for future claims over polar mineral, oil and gas deposits, and ice-free military ports.

Interest in Russia's remote regions increased after the independence of former Soviet republics in the 1990s. And the boom in Russian energy production in the 2000s further highlighted the lives of closed city economies and residents. Yet even for Russian artists, Norilsk, a closed city, required a creative form of documentation, a blurring of fact and fiction, exemplified in documentary film-maker Natalia Meshchaninova's docudrama *The Hope Factory*. A review of the film noted the significant barriers posed by filming in Novilsk:

> Being a center of the Gulag labor camps, Norilsk has evaded photographic and cinematic representation, and *The Hope Factory*, to a certain extent, reinstates the visibility of the city via the medium of film. Norilsk emerges as a character in its own right and, with its inescapable industrial chimneys and treeless wastelands, as an omnipresent and oppressive companion to youngsters struggling to deal with their place in the world.
>
> (Chefranova 2017)

While images of the secret city were shown to international film festival audiences, *The Hope Factory* was banned in Russia, owing to a 2014 law restricting profane language. Like Novikov's art/photography projects, Meshchaninova is known for blending fiction and the documentary form, a form of film-making that she believes enables a search for an authentic depiction of everyday life. To appease film censors, *The Hope Factory*'s producers asked Meshchaninova to reshoot portions of her film that contained profane language. Yet the process of re-staging an already fictionalized, yet spontaneous narrative met with resistance from the film-maker:

> My producers asked me to shoot a second take for each episode, making actors express themselves with different words. It was very complicated since I basically needed to shoot two films, and it was an additional pressure on actors who had to act each scene for a second time. When I began editing, I never thought specifically about obscene language as having the

purpose of surprising the viewer. I chose the filmed material that was the best and the most authentic, without any consideration of what words it contained. Some takes without obscene language happened to be better, true in terms of acting and rhythm, and they ended up in the final cut. For the actors, it was a task to speak as they might speak in real life, so the language belongs not merely to the characters, but to the actors as well. The actors did not need to learn specifically how to use that obscene language; they just had any limitations on speech removed. People of this age group often communicate with such language, no matter whether they are in Norilsk or in Moscow. When the producers requested a re-edit, nothing worked out: the takes without the foul language were worse and, as a result, it was a totally different film, sterilized in a way, a film that conveys a different meaning. Even if you cover obscene words with a beeping sound, your imagination will be provoked to produce something really shocking, way beyond what is actually used, and the outcome can be much more rude and vulgar, with my heroes immediately transformed into some trashy people. I completely rejected this idea of a second version of the film. There is only one version of *The Hope Factory*, and if the producers re-edit the film, I will remove my name from the credits.

(Chefranova 2017)

What few Norilsk-based films circulate, again often outside of Russian, almost always depicts this remote closed city as an inhospitable and environmentally toxic home. Yet, as early depictions of Soviet closed cities, inhabitants are commonly shown expressing pride in their city. One such documentary, produced for the American *Atlantic* magazine, leads off with a resident articulating the contradiction that seemingly defines this Arctic city: "It's deadly beautiful" (*The Atlantic* n.d.). Later in the film a man is shown walking next to an oil pipeline as strong wind gusts whip snow around in all directions. The resident says that this route "...opens up to a very beautiful view" as the camera pans to a wide image of factories and smokestacks. Another resident exclaims, as she gazes out over a large industrial landscape with multiple smokestacks, "Despite the brutality, factories, pipes, smoke, when there is no sun in winter, this is all so beautiful… I don't know how to explain it, but I want to photograph everything straight away" (ibid.).

Regardless of whether these are authentic opinions on the beauty of the toxic landscape, Novikov's *Norilskino* project demands more than vistas of this closed city. For Novikov, even the sporadic opening to foreign filmmakers cannot hide the media scarce scars on Norilsk's landscape. For Novikov, there is thus:

No need to live in Norilsk to see Norilsk. One of the most frequently filmed Russian cities has firmly settled in the visual memory of photography and film lovers thanks to constant updates. The coexistence of the industrial giant and human in specific urban and climatic conditions attracts filmmakers and photographers from around the world. Winter swimmers, panelki, permafrost, smoke from a chimney are the repeating patterns from year to year, circulated by documentary makers.

Like *ZATO*, *Norilskino* stages a photographic fiction, a faux film company that seeks to break out of the media scarce tundra, in so doing allowing "... the viewer to reflect on alternative modalities of the city's functioning, civic initiatives, and no less important, about the current state of photography, its status in the post-truth era" (Novikov n.d.).

Conclusions

With the help of Novikov's media scarce storytelling, his collaborative re-enactment and representation of life in a media restricted city paints a picture of economic experimentation, privilege, and environmental toxicity. Yet these are, to invoke Michel Foucault (1970), "histories of the present", staged performances informed by historical change, by a recognition of an evolved and porous secret city (that extends well beyond its borders). Secret cities are not faceless places. They constantly invoke secrecy and promise security, while largely serving citizens up as experimental subjects. To this end, the secret city's media scarcity is inherently economic. For even in Sailer's faceless spaces, human life lives on through economic activity, and the often toxic and desperate conditions that persist.

Media scarcity provided an economic cover, a shield for its residents. This is not to suggest that all residents supported the ban on photography and other media documentation of the secret city. In other words, the "privileges" of media scarcity were not uniformly appreciated by its residents. But the limits placed on the media documentation of the secret city (media scarcity) reaffirmed the exceptional nature of the secret city and its residents – its secretive work was deemed necessary for the very survival of the USSR and the "way of life" of secret city residents. Ironically, then, such media scarcity was designed to protect the future, by protecting the economic and military advantages produced in the secret city. Yet, the opposite is also on full display in the post-Soviet ZATO, where decades of scarce and sparse recognition (mediated or otherwise) of the toxic economic, environmental, and health impacts of the secret cities have only recently emerged.

Given the lack of media documentation of the secret city, lived, memorialized, humourous, contested, fictionalized, and forgotten stories and images of the secret city have emerged. In the absence of photos, film, and video of everyday life, the affective memories of residents loom large. There are few framed images to remind and otherwise anchor past lives to provide a backdrop to nostalgia, family, and place. Such a scarce media environment thus invites the kind of collaborative "theatrics" deployed by Novikov and his resident art collaborators throughout the pages of *ZATO*. Novikov's embodied politics of media scarcity re-enact and reinhabit the toxic life in the hopes of rewriting the scarce life as a hopeful future.

Notes

1. A 2019 study in the UK concluded that Enterprise Zones established since 2011 provided only one-third of the projected jobs. In some zones, employment dropped (Brockelbank and Mistry 2019).
2. Brock draws a historical parallel to the archipelago of Soviet gulags with the emergent "ZATO Archipelago". Novikov's 2019a art/photography "Norilskino" highlights the closed city Norilsk's past as a particularly notorious gulag (Novikov n.d.).

Bibliography

Beeston, Richard. 1995. "Russia Unveils 'Secret Cities' in Switch from Swords to Sofas." *Times* [London, England]. October 25, 1995.

Brock, Gregory. 1998. "Public Finance in the ZATO Archipelago." *Europe-Asia Studies* 50 (6): 1065–1081.

Brockelbank, Caroline, and Pritti Mistry. 2019. "Enterprise Zones 'Failed to Deliver' Jobs Boost in England." *BBC*. July 11. Accessed March 5, 2020. https://www.bbc.com/news/uk-england-48856440.

Brown, Kate. 2013. *Nuclear Families, Atomic Cities, and the Great Soviet and American Plutonium Disasters*. Oxford: Oxford University Press.

Chefranova, Oksana. 2017. Interview. "Towards Poetics of Authenticity: *The Hope Factory* and the New Wave of Russian Women Filmmakers. A Conversation with Natalia Meschaninova." *Apparatus. Film, Media and Digital Cultures in Central and Eastern Europe* 4. https://doi.org/10.17892/app.2017.0004.71.

Easterling, Keller. 2014. *Extrastatecraft: The Power of Infrastructure Space*. London: Verso.

Foucault Michel. 1970. *The Order of Things: An Archaeology of the Human Sciences*. London: Tavistock.

Glazunov, Mikhail. 2016. *Corporate Strategy in Post-Communist Russia*. London: Routledge.

Goetschel, Samira. 2005. *Secret City: The Oak Ridge Story - The War Years*. Arlington VA: PBS.

Goetschel, Samira. 2016. *City 40*. D.I.G. Films.

Kaspar-Eisert, Verena. 2023. *Preface, Sailer, Gregor*. Unseen Places, Vienna: Kehrer, pp. 9–11.

Masterman, Sue. 1998. "Russia's Secret Cities in Silicone Valley Deal." *Evening Standard*, September 23, p. 20.

Novikov, Sergey. 2019a. *ZATO*, 2nd edition. Moscow: Books Recurrent.

Novikov, Sergey. 2019b. "Closer than Switzerland." Accessed November 28, 2022. https://sergeynovikov.com/closerthanswitzerland/.

Novikov, Sergey. n.d. "Norilskkino." Accessed November 28, 2022. https://sergeynovikov.com/norilskkinotext/.

Riabov, Oleg, and Tatiana Riabova. 2014. "The Remasculinization of Russia?: Gender, Nationalism, and the Legitimation of Power under Vladimir Putin." *Problems of Post-Communism* 61 (2): 23–35.
Sailer, Gregor. 2012. *Closed Cities*. Heidelberg: Kehrer Press.
Sailer, Gregor. 2022. "Unseen Places". Exhibition. Accessed March 1, 2023. https://www.kunsthauswien.com/en/exhibitions/unseen-places/.
Sailer, Gregor. 2023. *Unseen Places*. Vienna: Kehrer.
Sailer, Gregor. n.d. "Photography." Accessed December 1, 2023. https://gregorsailer.com/Projects.
Shiklomanov, Nikolay I., and Marlene Laruelle. 2017. "A Truly Arctic City: An Introduction to the Special Issue on the City of Norilsk, Russia." *Polar Geography* 40 (4): 251–256.
Sixsmith, Martin. 2010. *Putin's Oil: The Yukos Affair and the Struggle for Russia*. London: Continuum.
The Atlantic. n.d. "Would You Live in This Toxic, Closed-Off City?" Accessed November 22, 2022. https://www.youtube.com/watch?v=ks9E9XQp_2k.

5 Bunker media

Messages from the abundant and redundant underground

To live an underground life is to fly under the radar, to live off the grid, to hide, resist, and/or take on another persona. Underground life is exceptional; it is far from the norm. The underground is typically defined by its opposition to the mainstream. But while some choose to go underground as a lifestyle choice, others are forced to do so. Regardless, an underground life is one where actions and identities are typically hidden, masked, or sheltered from the social and political gaze. Underground lives are for the most part precarious lives.

But the underground is also a place of culture, resistance, imagination, storytelling, and myth building. The underground is a liminal space where provocative and controversial ideas, actions, and behaviours are launched into the mainstream. Yet as largely secretive and subversive places, the underground is rarely, if ever, fully mediated, that is, subject to the full glare of the media industries. Stories of the underground are thus largely *post mediated*, emerging years after their heyday. Underground life is therefore *media scarce*, meaning it initially resists widespread media capture and dissemination. By comparison today, the very opposite dynamic seems to prevail: an abundant media culture, fuelled by social media platforms and handheld media devices, seemingly demands the sharing of ever more intimate and granular aspects of their everyday lives – every meal, party, haircut, and vacation. This raises the question of how past media scarce and underground lives are mediated, or rather post mediated. How do former underground dwellers tell their stories in the present given their media scarce past, that is, without media documents?

It would be a mistake, however, to restrict the demands of an abundant media culture to migrants, refugees, prisoners, or other marginalized and media scarce communities who have been displaced from their homes, gone underground into hiding, or been incarcerated. Media scarce communities typically have gaps in their personal media histories and might subsequently be hard-pressed to tell their stories without the aid of family videos or photos that document their past. In this chapter, we question if these underground and media scarce lives are limited to exceptional experiences, to specific marginalized and precarious communities. We argue that the precarity posed by media scarcity – of potentially being disconnected – was once generalized and made a universal threat during the cold war period of the 1950s and 1960s. During this period in time, heightened by the Cuban missile crisis and fuelled by a pervasive ideological battle, citizens lived under threat of nuclear annihilation, and consequently were encouraged to seek cover, under tables, desks, chairs, or preferably underground.

Here in this chapter, we turn to that infamous place of atomic age last resort, the bunker. Unlike the "underground" life of deep subculture, underground life in the literal sense of subterranean survival involves a different relationship between scarcity and abundance. The underground might serve as a place to store preserves, but we would be hard-pressed to imagine it as a place of bounty and prosperity as it was in the Tarde novel we saw in Chapter 1. Despite being a place of scarcity, bunkers paradoxically speak to abundant life through their very redundancy. Indeed, apocalyptic austerity can only be mitigated through abundant preparation. For instance, the diligent prepper must continually replenish vast stores of perishable canned food – never to be used for their dedicated purpose yet standing reserve. Similarly, the communication technologies housed in bunkers are marked by inherent redundancy and a need to be tested, upgraded, and replaced so long as the escalating threat of apocalypse persists, pushing once cutting-edge technologies into obsolescence – typically before they were even operationally needed.

During the height of the cold war, bunkers were domesticated, sold as extensions of the comfortable, consumer-abundant, media home. But the existential threat of nuclear war could not contain the entrenched assumption of abundance, which we could comfortably carry on under threat of – or indeed after – nuclear war. Rather, as we shall detail, cold war-era bunkers (particularly military ones) were increasingly made media-redundant, but not in the sense that they were wasteful or inefficient. Following Parikka (2012) and others, redundancy is "…not just an unwanted element…but a more defining feature…" (91). While bunkers were indeed flush with media, the hope was that they would never have to be used. Indeed, cold war bunkers were never fully operationalized. The redundant bunker promised a dystopic fail-safe future, where one would be seemingly protected from nuclear fallout, yet likely never able to return to the earth's surface again. Thus, as institutions, buildings, and architectures, cold war bunkers were more than abundant; they did more than replicate the aspirations of a consumer media culture, and they displaced the harsh realities of a sustained if not persistent underground life by insisting that the horror of its occupation and full operation would ultimately deter its intended use. The bunker resisted the precarity of a media scarce past and future; it became media – a redundant form of *bunker media*.

In this chapter, we demonstrate how the generalized condition of precarity once articulated by the existential threat of the cold war gave rise to a strategy of media redundancy that throws the politics of media scarcity into sharp relief. Redundancy semantically highlights the central problematic of our book in exposing the injustices and inequalities that arise within a media culture marked by scarcity in abundance. Redundancy speaks to what is "overflowing" and "surging up" but is used to describe what is deemed not useful or unneeded. Thus, we suggest that redundancy can serve as a red flag about the values and politics that are imposed when decisions are made about what should be considered essential or not within a culture of abundance. Today, media abundance is arguably predicated on increasing *human redundancy*, for example, as generative artificial intelligence (AI) becomes positioned to replace or supplement human workers, spurring concerns of massive lay-offs and greater precarity in creative industries. Perhaps in the future, we will have more stories in circulation but far greater precarity within our storytelling communities. Similarly, during the cold war, the engineered redundancy of bunker media served to mediate geopolitical tensions without proper regard for the protection and continuity of human life or other social concerns. In other words, bunker media was designed to ensure that government and military leadership could wage and withstand nuclear war while leaving its governed subjects left to their own scarce devices.

Given its location, sandwiched in between the two cold war adversaries, the USSR and the USA, the chapter's focus on Canadian bunker media is not arbitrary. As many canonical media scholars have noted (Innis 1927, 2008; McLuhan 1964; McLuhan and Powers 1989), Canadian space and technology have often served to *mediate* geopolitical tensions and economies. The Canadian bunker is no different in this respect, offering a stark contrast to more expansive, secretive, and embedded bunkers in many other parts of the world, including, of course, the USA. Unlike the superpowers to its north and south, Canada built a relatively modest bunker infrastructure, anchored by the federal government's so-called "Diefenbunker", named after cold war-era prime minister John Diefenbaker. The Diefenbunker was widely known to the public as a semi-submerged installation that maintained communications to other cold war defence installations and infrastructure. In short, as a central node in the modest Canadian bunker network, its main role was to communicate Canadian military readiness to friend and foe. The Diefenbunker thus serves as prototypical bunker media, an installation and technology that sought to reassure a stable governed future that protected the *identity* of its national subjects, as opposed to Canadian civilian lives. Bunker media would not be media scarce. Yet after the bunker was decommissioned and renovated into Canada's Cold War Museum, we question its continued redundant media power. Without the threat of global thermonuclear war, what myth of universal abundance can the post mediated and post-cold war bunker now communicate from the underground?

The genesis of bunkerology

Bunkers have long told stories about their role in past, present, and future military conflicts. Yet critics have also noted that bunkers obscure their own location and form. Paul Virilio's (1994a) part essay, part photography book, *Bunker Archaeology*, captures this point succinctly through the practice of "bunkerology", or finding, unearthing, and capturing (typically with photography) largely hidden or otherwise obscured cement military bunkers. Not surprisingly, the cultural power of bunkers has often been framed as an architectural phenomenon, particularly in its entropic form, as ruins. John Beck's (2011) influential essay on the bunker complex consequently focuses on the ambivalence of its materiality, as an architectural form that resists categorization. Moreover, for the bunker to be "effective", Beck argued it *needed* to be hidden, lest it become redundant (86), seemingly in the literal sense, as a building devoid of purpose. Curiously, Beck sets aside Virilio's facilitation with military technologies as forms of media. Virilio emphasizes the materiality of the bunker as a distinct semi-submerged architectural form of "military surface infrastructure" (12) and its invocation of "bad memories…[and] many fantasies too" (13), helping to frame bunker media as both infrastructure and storytelling device, not merely as hidden underground tomb.

In naming his book an "Archaeology", Virilio defined bunkers as distinct artefacts, ruins, and decaying structures – "one of the rare modern monolithic architectures" (37). Yet time and again, he returned to the bunker as mediating architecture. Flintham (2020), by contrast, argues for a return to a geology of bunkers, in part because cold war bunkers were never fully inhabited or used for their designed purpose, a definition of redundancy more befitting the goals of this chapter. He argues that "very few studies relate to bunkers without humans" (Flintham 2020, 12). To be sure, the cold war bunker, and indeed its Second World War antecedents were overdetermined by their concrete materiality, a substance that while reaffirming and reinforcing its role as shelter also produced a distinctly cold, environmentally bleak and unnatural space of inhabitation. Vanderbilt (2002, 6) captures this succinctly when referring to the bunker as "a pure representation of function in poured concrete". Such perspectives have become increasingly relevant for organizations engaged to reopen, renovate, and redesign cold war-era bunkers, since these structures are also "filled with sensitive and delicate organised objects and a terrifying array of largely unstable plastics, rubbers and painted surfaces" (Bowers and Booth 2017, 205–206).

We suggest though, following Klinke (2018, vii) that while bunkers are indeed overdetermined by their distinct subterranean architecture, concrete "is difficult to categorise – it almost wants to be interpreted". While bunkers share a monolithic concrete form and environment, Kinnear (2020) importantly notes that they were built using mass-produced designs and products.

Hence, he argues that such common architectural formats and spaces are flexible and adaptable to new technologies, a point we return to during our concluding discussion of the reopening of bunkers as sites of participatory play. The bunker was mediated beyond concrete and subterranean walls, its stories extended far and beyond the sheltered site. Indeed, bunkers often served a networked role. Richemond-Barak (2018, 66) argues that the bunker operated alongside satellite, spy plane, and drone surveillance, implicated in the "vertical axis of surveillance". For instance, in the UK, military bunkers were built to anchor regional zones that facilitated military command and control functions (Cocroft and Thomas 2004, 199), and were later updated to include weather and fallout sensors (Bennett 2017, 3; Flintham 2020, 15).

Thus, as semi-submerged military and communication nodes, bunkers were never fully secret nor fully "underground" facilities. Rather they were typically "hiding in plain sight", as Bennett argues (2017, 5), layered vertically. The visibility of such installations thus made bunkers fodder for anti-nuke protests around the world, particularly in the UK where opposition grew to US-based military personnel and nuclear weapons (5). In addition to campaigns that sought to normalise domestic bunkers during the height of the cold war (Masco 2009; Rose 2001), urban cold war bunkers – meant to protect larger numbers of city dwellers in urban cores – were redesigned to integrate seamlessly into the urban landscape. For instance, Klinke (2018) notes that cold war bunkers were renovated into parking garages, hotels, and subway stations. In short, military planners "blended the bunker into the urban fabric" (71). Just as cities became fortified, incorporating bunkers into transportation hubs and subterranean parking lots, bunkers also became part of communications and media systems. Military bunkers were not simply secret hidden concrete structures; they were technologies built to mediate, to tell stories.

Installations that, on the surface, were perceived as highly secretive were rather, particularly in the case of Canada, well known to the press. Canadian *bunker media*, as we shall discuss, in both the past and the present, negotiated existential anxieties about the underground, about being media scarce. Yet bunkers offered more than abundant media, not simply the creature comforts and mediated class anxieties about keeping up with neighbours. Bunker media extended outwards by radio waves and buried landlines to government and military officials, to the North American Aerospace Defense Command (NORAD), to enemies, to television and cinematic screens, and to citizens. Bunker media connected to early warning systems *such* as the Distant Early Warning or DEW line, to weather stations, to fallout sensors, and to other communications nodes. Bunker media was fused with the life-threatening realities of nuclear war and life-saving imaginaries nurtured by continuity of government (COG) planners and (re)performed by dutiful citizens who built domestic fallout shelters, stocked food and water, and stood ready by their radios. Abundant preparation for an underground existence, we might say. Today, bunker media in many places around the world continues to communicate, not as hollow ruins or containers of obsolete technology but as media that tell stories of our past, (re)performing apocalyptic anxieties and confronting potential future existential threats. And as we become increasingly dependent on media abundance, the spectre of bunker life looms all the larger.

Canada as the front line of the apocalypse

Canadian bunker media may seem peripheral. Why focus on Canada given its proximity to a superpower steeped in cold war mythologies, ideologies, and, well, bunkers? One could conduct a rather compelling study of American bunker media, given that the former presidential bunker in Washington DC now serves as an archive of treasured celluloid films (GBS 2016). Many other countries that suffered large-scale military bombardments, such as Vietnam, Germany, the USSR, and the UK, also have extensive civilian and military bunker histories (McCamley 2016; Ozorak 2012; Stokes 2017). Much less discussed though is Canada's unique geographic position in the cold war, as effectively the front line in the nuclear standoff between the United States and the Soviet Union. Beyond serving as a site of nuclear missile testing (Clearwater 2006), Canada's cold war role was mostly viewed as defensive and informational, as the site of an early warning radar system.

Marshall McLuhan (1964) saw the DEW line – sixty-three missile tracking radar stations that formed a line across the Canadian Arctic – as a cultural metaphor, a system that mediated not only Canada's place in the geopolitical world but its potential future (Lajeunesse 2007). McLuhan (1969) wrote: "I think of art, at its most significant, as a DEW line, a Distant Early Warning system that can always be relied upon to tell the old culture what is beginning to happen to it". Such an early warning system would frame stories that foretold the future in much the same way that underground politics and culture would usher into the mainstream, and, moreover, how Canada's underground would become a key site in its plans for passive civil defence (Campbell 2017).

Yet it is through the redundancy of bunker media, as an essential infrastructure that would hopefully never have to be needed, that the dangers and precarity of the underground were mediated. Typically, the underground is understood as a place of relative disconnection from general society or business as usual; the underground is also typically marked by cultural disconnection from a regime of media abundance that claims to be expansive and durable but may in fact be increasingly viewed as impossible to sustain in the wake of ecological collapse. Moreover, disconnection is arguably what gives underground subcultures their subversive potential. In contrast, conservative bunker media made the underground into an extension of mainstream abundant ideology and communications infrastructure. As the front line of the apocalypse, the cold war underground could no longer be a place of disconnection and of media scarcity but a place of redundancy. Today, bunker media creates an opportunity to question where the front line is today. For instance, in the face of irreversible climate catastrophe, what role does the underground play? What politics of media scarcity are available for the sake of resistance, survival, and collective mobilization? Where and how can underground voices resurface to disrupt the regime of abundance and insatiable capitalist hunger that threatens to swallow up all life on earth today?

With the Soviet Union's detonation of their first atomic bomb in 1949 and the beginning of the Korean War in 1950, cold war nuclear anxieties renewed concerns about civil defence in Canada. After the first successful tests of American and Soviet hydrogen bombs in 1952 and 1955, the devastating potential of thermonuclear war could no longer be ignored. During this growing international crisis, Canadian Prime Minister John Diefenbaker publicly announced in 1958 that "development of a decentralised federal system of emergency government with central, regional and zonal elements would proceed" (Panneton 2015). Thus began, what we posit, as the beginning of the abundant, bunker-media project, of domesticating bunker infrastructure within the confines of the home and other everyday places. Bunker media attempted a gradual creative rebrand of the underground from a place of isolation to a redundant infrastructure.

In 1954, prior to Diefenbaker's public announcement concerning emergency government plans, studies of the effects of thermonuclear war from the US Atomic Energy Commission had revealed alarming effects of radiation fallout (McConnell 1998, Chapter 1, 8), disclosures that transformed the basis for civil defence planning in Canada. Although properly constructed buildings could indeed withstand the blast of an atomic bomb, meaning that basement shelters could provide sufficient safety to citizens in target cities, a policy of temporarily seeking shelter was deemed useless in protecting against the more devastating power of hydrogen bombs. Consequently, a federal public relations campaign was launched to instruct the public about the importance of building fallout shelters near or under their homes to help increase their odds of survival. Unlike previous publicity plans that had concentrated on a handful of cities across the country, the national survival plan now emphasised that all citizens would have to take on the responsibility to defend their families. As Figure 5.1 shows, citizens were admonished not to ignore the threat of thermonuclear war by ignorantly sticking their heads in the ground (Government of Canada n.d.).

Going underground

Preparations for nuclear fallout came in the form of plans for underground life. Citizens were obliged to materially imagine and prepare for living underground, digging in to inhabit the subterranean strata, as we see in the Diefenbaker government issued *Your Basement Fallout Shelter: Blueprint for*

Figure 5.1 Canadian civil defence poster, circa 1950.

Survival No. 1 (Government of Canada 1961). The flyer provided a detailed construction outline of the basement fallout shelter as a "do-it-yourself" project (6), notably an *extension of the home*, specifically in the basement. While the home bunker is shown to be rather sparse in drawings in the "Blueprint for Survival", a radio is given prominence in two images. Bunker media, in Canada at least, was an extension of the abundant home, a temporary space of shelter.

While domestic Canadian bunkers were framed as limited extensions or renovations of the home, American campaigns produced more elaborate plans of backyard installations that included all the creature comforts of home, including plentiful media. Boyer (2005, x) attributes this difference to how the American public, after some initial resistance, came to largely accept the tangible threat of nuclear war during the cold war, becoming part of the "fabric of the culture" (xviii). Boyer argues that this cultural agenda was a deliberate effort by the US government, prompted by psychological and sociological research, to deploy elaborate civil defence preparedness as a means of regulating atomic anxiety and mass hysteria.

The confluence of abundant conspicuous consumer culture, an omnipresent anti-communist ideology, and the beginnings of suburban middle-class life are foregrounded in nearly every American government film produced about the dangers of nuclear war. Produced from early cold war government films, the documentary classic *The Atomic Café* (1982) emphasized both the comforts and fears of the time. Images of suburban ice cream trucks and dinner at the family table are juxtaposed against images of armed conflicts and mushroom clouds. Ultimately the call to protect the family and the way of life prevails, under cover, under the school desk, and in the family bunker. Even contemporary images of luxurious bunkers today invoke and revisit the abundant bunker media of 1950s America. A widely used Getty archive drawing of a family striking an early evening living room pose shows a child sprawled on the floor of the backyard bunker reading from a pile of books, while her parents hover over a turntable presumably debating the sound quality of a Miles Davis LP. Except for some well-hidden tools, cranks and pulleys, the bunker could be a credible – meaning clichéd – representation of the idealized, white suburban 1950s home. As the cold war deepened, however, images of the media abundant, semi-detached domestic bunker would give way to more explicitly militarized bunkers, which promised the future of the state through layers of redundant media and communications infrastructure.

As an existential threat to the national identity, Canadian bunker media focused on convincing citizens that the state, government, and its leadership would be protected in the event of nuclear war. In short, there would be a Canada and Canadians in a post-nuclear future. In 1959, sites for a permanent COG headquarters were surveyed (Maloney 2012, 47). Consisting of underground and aboveground components, the initial plan was to construct three interconnected fallout-proof bunkers upwind of Ottawa to house the core of federal government decision-makers, including the Prime Minister and cabinet, the Governor General, several Supreme Court Justices, the Royal

Canadian Mounted Police (RCMP) Commissioner, the Federal Civil Defence Coordinator, and a skeleton bureaucracy drawn from each government department (47). Following several evaluations and to accommodate budget limitations, a compromise was reached: the design of the COG headquarters or CEGHQ (Central Emergency Government Headquarters), initially conceived as three underground buildings – an executive centre, an administrative centre, and a communications centre – was modified to consist of one large bunker and three antenna farms, one of which included an underground transmitter facility (48–49). This facility located at Canadian Forces Station Carp, approximately 40 km west from Ottawa's Parliament Hill, is Canada's largest cold war-era bunker, popularly known as the "Diefenbunker": a massive four-storey underground shelter constructed between 1959 and 1961.

The Diefenbunker paradoxically functioned as both an ongoing symbol to the public about COG preparedness and a secretive military installation, Canadian Forces Station Carp. During its roughly thirty-three years of active defence use (1961–1994), the Diefenbunker's top-secret communications was operated by a staff of 100–150 people on 24/7 rotating shifts (Diefenbunker Museum n.d.-a). The bunker supplies were meant to accommodate a month-long period of lockdown, adequate rations for 535 personnel (Diefenbunker Museum n.d.-a). Occupying about 100,000 square feet, the bunker consists of four underground storeys with 350 rooms, including a decontamination chamber, a war room, medical facilities, dining spaces, and dormitories (Panneton 2015). Protected by its location in a natural valley, the structure was designed to resist a 5-megaton nuclear weapon detonation just over a mile away (Defence Construction Canada n.d.).

Although the site's primary protection and operational security derived from a principle of concealment and secrecy, followed by the physical protection afforded by the structure itself (Maloney 2012, 48), public scrutiny of the Diefenbunker was swift, compromising its surreptitious defences even before construction was complete. An official army press release on August 6, 1959 stated the COG planners cover story for the site's construction: "The Canadian Army has received approval to construct an Experimental Army Signals Establishment in the area of Carp, Almonte, and Arnprior. This will involve a number of transmitting and receiving facilities and buildings to service them" (Maloney 2012, 49). However, following an alleged leak, a full exposé of the bunker was published in the *Ottawa Citizen* in April 1961 speculating that the Carp facility was to be used as a COG relocation facility for government leadership (Campbell 1961). Subsequently, in September, the *Toronto Telegram* published a photograph of the unfinished construction site taken from a private plane, along with a headline "This is the Diefenbunker!" (Toronto Telegram 1961). Reporters canvassed locals in Carp and inaccurately reported that the facility was a three-level structure that stretched 80-foot underground (Maloney 2012, 49). The bunker thus became both mediated and medium.

Diefenbunker media

At the outset of construction, there was widespread recognition that the Diefenbunker would be effectively rendered "useless without communications" (Maloney 2012, 48). Significant redundancies in the communications infrastructure were integrated into the network to ensure the integrity of its communication channels, including redundant landline telephones, teleprinters, transmitters, receivers, and cryptography machines. "Dispersion, not hardening, was the key here" (48).[1] The Diefenbunker was in effect designed as an underground media hub. COG planners would have certainly preferred to more robustly defend the communications infrastructure of what was officially referred to as PROJECT EASE, the central node of its bunker network. However, the finalized plan reflected the aforementioned economic compromise taken by the Canadian Government: instead of having "several dispersed underground sites across the Ottawa Valley area, each with its own main communications suite and a backup" (48–49), in the end, only one large underground building was constructed along with three scattered antenna farms, one of which included an underground transmitter facility.[2] The Diefenbunker, would consequently mediate its redundancy vertically, reserving each floor for different operations.

One notable exception to the internal verticalization of Diefenbunker media was the introduction of the US-Canada missile tracking system. As part of the NORAD agreement, the "ICONORAMA" was installed in 1961 in the operations centre at the Diefenbunker (Johannesson 2011). The ICONORAMA consisted of an electronic map projected in a control room "theatre".[3] The system visualized a synthesis of surveillance information collected from NORAD radar stations, interceptor squadrons, missile sites, space tracking and ballistic missile warning units, United States' Strategic Air Command, naval forces off both coasts, the Pentagon, and the Department of National Defence (DND) in Canada (USAADS 1965, Chapter 2, 18). The system operated by reading encrypted teletype messages of target information sent by NORAD computers at Colorado Springs COG and visualized this on the theatre screen to allow for continuous observation of the direction of travel of aerospace and seaborne vessels over any area of the continent monitored by its surveillance networks (18).

As a theatre display for mapping in near real time, the global arms trajectory of nuclear war, the ICONORAMA served as a unique form of underground, bunker media – one that coupled the vertical militarized form of surveillance, extensively detailed by Stephen Graham (2016), with iconic images of war rooms projected onto cinematic screens by Hollywood. For the North Atlantic Treaty Organization (NATO) such subterranean projections helped to facilitate COG authorities' desire for a complete, real-time picture of aerial activity from the darkness and remoteness of the underground bunker. The ICONORAMA would have provided Canadian COG authorities with a front row seat to a live representation of the end of the world. On the other hand, it also functioned according to a logic of semi-submerged mediation, as yet another technological symbol of government and military preparedness, which, first, challenged and perhaps dissuaded the threat of nuclear war and, second, potentially assured the Canadian population that their survival was being taken seriously by COG planners insofar as the bunker was designed to mediate potential nuclear threats (missiles). This is illustrated by American and Canadian advertisements and news stories concerning the ICONORAMA dating between 1959 and 1961 showcasing the technology to the public (Ling-Temco Electronics 1961; Ottawa Journal 1961, 18). We are particularly struck by one advertisement which depicts the ICONORAMA theatre display superimposed over an image of the globe from a satellite perspective and features enemy missiles speeding towards North America with their trajectories neatly plotted in red and monitored by a calm and professionally composed staff. The heading reads: "BMEWS [Ballistic Missile Early Warning System] SPACE SURVEILLANCE" (VMWARA n.d.). Here we can assert that the abundant computer systems, visualizing technology, and broader communication media of the Canadian bunker network not only physically extended beyond the subterranean structures of bunkers, even as far as the earth's orbit, but also implicated the entire globe within the theatrical screen of its constituting COG imaginary.

Bunkers remediated

As the threat of nuclear attack gradually receded from public consciousness in Canada after the fall of the Berlin Wall, the semi-submerged and redundant logic of its bunker network has survived, albeit, in adapted forms. The full ICONORAMA system is notably one of the select few bunker media components left out of the decommissioned Diefenbunker, renovated in 1998 to house Canada's Cold War Museum. A rather low-tech version of the system is currently presented to museum visitors. While other forms of bunker media continue to be exhibited in the museum, including an active ham radio station, a Canadian Broadcasting Corporation (CBC) radio station, and a room filled with computer servers, the ICONORAMA remains elusive, a classified topic by the Canadian government. However, with the end of the cold war, and the renovation of the Diefenbunker and other similar installations worldwide (Kinnear 2020; Wilson 2020), bunker media – including their cinematic representations (Maloney 2020) – have only grown in prominence, offering customized, gamified, or artistic reflections on contemporary anxieties, precarious conditions, and future challenges.

Although the average citizen may be unaware or perhaps have forgotten about Canada's bunkers (Manning 2003; Matthews and Anstett 2015), their ongoing costs to government and potential for redevelopment have begun to receive more attention by news organizations and documentary film-makers (CTV News 2015; Deachman 2022; Ottawa Citizen 2018; TBTV 2021). Much attention has focused on the aforementioned archaeology of bunkers, that is, as a form of bunkerology. Yet given the scale of such installations, particularly in the case of the Diefenbunker, new business models for the concrete underground have flourished. Subsequently, in the remainder of the chapter, we discuss the redesign of bunker media (Strömberg 2013) into a site of entertainment that cautiously – or sometimes not – remediates existential threats in the concrete substrata. We ask how contemporary bunker media narrates its nuclear-era past and potential futures, how it seeks to maintain the cold war tensions of redundant bunker media, within a museum seemingly bursting at the seams with abundant media programming. How do exhibitions, events, and programmes speak about past, present, and future existential threats of visiting, playing, and learning in the underground?

While the cold war Diefenbunker media embraced a redundant technological imaginary to layer its protective infrastructure and communicate its never-to-be-used preparedness, the contemporary remediated Diefenbunker, Canada's Cold War Museum, now revels in its excess, entertainment, and abundance – arguably to the point of decadence. To welcome visitors, secrecy, fear, and media scarcity are invoked, yet distanced beyond the realm of redundancy to a form of novel curiosity. The revitalized Diefenbunker museum mediates its past redundancy while amplifying its multipurpose space as an event-like hall. Writing about the Diefenbunker museum, Schneider (2010, 66) likewise observes how the "content and status of the site becomes a showroom rather than a secret container for nuclear doom". Klinke's (2018, 111–112) study of German cold war bunkers similarly foretold this turn to playful bunker media, a shift that increasingly focuses on the bunker visitor's experience. Notions of play were central to military discourses and technological simulations of nuclear war and its subsequent radioactive fallout. Klinke (2018) wrote that "[the simulation] was variously described in official sources as an 'exercise', 'play', 'nuclear play' or a game with 'players'…a 'crap game' yet…the game did not allow for negotiations with the Soviet Union…the only goal was the smooth release of nuclear weapons rather than the prevention of war" (114). Other playful accounts of the bunker served distinct propagandistic purposes: West German news reports of nuclear war simulations noted the consumption of alcohol and night-time parties in bunkers. These were seized upon by East German Stasi agents who framed the West German bunker as a space of excessive drinking and sexual harassment: "In effect the bunker was turned into a space of subterranean luxury, excessive/non-consensual sexuality and forbidden political enjoyment" (Klinke 2018, 115). Reviews of the Diefenbunker's current website and active social media accounts (particularly Instagram) likewise force us to rethink bunker media through creative industries like framework, where visitor experience, through the consumption of alcohol, gamified museum experiences and children's holiday camp programming mix with stories of nuclear annihilation and cold war subterfuge in an exceptionally well-maintained, time capsule like four-storey underground bunker.[4]

Enter the bunker

The surface of the Diefenbunker site itself retains a decidedly sparse air of desertion, of a military site left to ossify. There is minimal museum-like signage at the entrance of the bunker, leaving the visitor to navigate a long imposing blast tunnel that eventually leads to the museum's ticket desk. Visitors pass through a biohazard shower to enter the museum and bunker, setting an air of authenticity to the beginning of the visitor experience. Much of the first underground floor of the bunker is similarly focused on matters of survival, health, and decontamination. The remaining underground floors, however, tell a rather different story, the next level down houses government and media operations, including the aforementioned CBC radio station that includes a DJ-like studio replete with turntable and vinyl collection still in play. The entire floor is reminiscent of a drab government building, albeit with smaller offices and no windows. The same is true for the next deeper level, where visitors will find a large cafeteria that looks much like any other institutional lunch-time canteen.

It is only when one arrives at the Diefenbunker's deepest level that visitors are faced with the starkest contrast between the mediation of a cold war-era bunker and a remediated museum and event space. Unlike the other floors, the 100-level feels like a basement. This last level includes a space for the storage of provisions and a morgue. Down a long passageway, one finds the sparsest and most physically protected room in the bunker, the Bank of Canada vault, designed to hold gold bullion. The museum's website offers a short history of the room:

> In the event of a nuclear attack on North America, Canada would need to protect their gold reserves so they could have a form of currency to rebuild the country. If gold were to become irradiated it would lose its value, so it made it essential to protect it from radiation. With that in mind, the Canadian government spared no expense in building the Bank of Canada Vault.
> (Diefenbunker Museum 2019)

The door to the room resembles most bank vaults; it is at least two or three feet thick. Located in the most fortified and secure location of the Diefenbunker, the massive store of gold reminds us that COG planners believed that post-nuclear economic abundance should be prioritized above all else – even, of course, human life.

In the newly renovated and reimagined bunker media, the space now serves as an art gallery – one of the few permanent spaces that explicitly communicate through its programming the tension between cold war narratives and the museum's programming that rearticulates the existential danger of nuclear war into a media-abundant, gamified form of play. The gallery's mandate is to bring together cold war themes and contemporary issues of national concern, such as Indigenous reconciliation (Diefenbunker 2021). Mairi Brascoupé's recent residence, for instance, explored "our understanding of place during times of change and uncertainty and how values differ, specifically for Indigenous people, through mapping and remapping during Canada's Cold War history" (Diefenbunker Museum n.d.-b). Further, a newly announced installation from Christos Pantieras "will draw inspiration from the intersection of 2SLGBTQ+ history and experience, to amplify important stories from the Cold War that continue to impact lives today" (ibid.). Demonstrating more variety in programming, a series of musical concerts that feature underground punk aesthetics were also buried in the deep recesses of the vault, imagining its inescapable concrete environs as a perfect place to host a "graffiti wall" (DMI 2018). Today, the Diefenbunker's cold war politics of media scarcity, its values and problems, are obscured, as the underground becomes a showroom for underground culture.

Much of the new bunker media promoted by the museum, however, inhabits spaces closer to the bunker's surface, far away from its deeper, underground cold war origins. The bunker's unique history and design often merely serves as a novelty backdrop to event hall-like programming (Diefenbunker n.d.-d), for instance, as host to an annual whiskey tasting fundraiser (DMI 2015). An advertisement for the event – depicting drinking and dancing – could just as easily have been located at a dance hall or hotel ballroom. Highlighting ludic appeal, a zombie walk is promoted in the blast tunnel (DMI 2017, 2018), an existential threat more commonly found on HBO.

In the years preceding the COVID pandemic, the Diefenbunker museum, looking for more sources of revenue, partnered with an Ottawa-based company to promote the "world's largest escape room" (Diefenbunker Museum n.d.-c). With different themes each year, the escape room seemed at first to be a rather odd entertainment model to incorporate into the bunker; but as a form of bunker media, it succeeds again in individualising the experience of the space for the visitor-player. While the escape games draw upon multi-mediated narratives and player tasks that seek to upend a catastrophic thermonuclear end of the world scenario, ultimately, as prototypical underground bunker media, the escape room asks the key question of underground denizens: "Will you make it out of the bunker?" (Diefenbunker Museum n.d.-c).

Conclusion

Stepping out of the Diefenbunker, let us similarly ask, what messages radiate from its concrete walls, its overdetermined history, and its redundant design? What does this underground say about its displaced, precarious, and at-risk population, the challenges of media scarcity? Unlike those who have been forced underground to avoid persecution, such subterranean conditions have been intensely mediatized as redundant, abundant, excessive, or otherwise "decadent" spaces (Keane 2013). Yet, at the same time, the concrete underground cannot escape its distinct function and purpose, as a shelter and site of survival, as a decidedly media scarce place. It is therefore left to bunker media to communicate, signal, and prompt us to imagine the possibility of never returning to the surface or re-entering a community and society. Bunker media thus tell stories, part of which requires a degree of reassurance, normalcy, domesticity, and protection, while another part, kept redundant, projects a grim reality of annihilation or a media scarce underground where stories are entombed within a concrete enclosure.

Cold war bunker media sought to straddle the line between publicity and secrecy to reassure and protect, while also warning about the effects of radioactive fallout and global thermonuclear war. To be more than a site of survival, bunkers – both domestic and military – needed to be networked and connected through various channels to other sites and sources of information. Rather than being abundant and plentiful, we argue that the cold war bunker media was redundant – such networks contained layers of redundancy, channels, wires, networks, and notes that would only be used in the case of failure of primary systems. Redundancy assured that hope could be preserved, that an exit from the underground could at least be imagined if not lived.

In the newly remediated museum and event hall bunker, layers of redundancy have been replaced by institutional redundancy, meaning that the bunker was never put into full use – bunker media was never fully activated as a lifeline. Stripped of its efficacy and design, bunker media has consequently morphed from a redundant life-dependent system to a platform and space of play. Some aspects of Diefenbunker media speculate about the broader politics of the underground, of contrasting identities, conflict, and past injustices, as is evidenced by the compelling gallery programming, albeit restricted to the secure vault in the very basement of the bunker. Yet as a whole, stripped of its primary, redundant infrastructure, bunker media has increasingly reverted to the materiality of its underground space to find and articulate new, renewed, and largely fictionalized existential threats.

As of Fall 2022, the Diefenbunker has yet to acknowledge the re-emergence of cold war tensions, including most notably nuclear threats made by Russian president Vladimir Putin. The pummelling of large areas of Ukraine has once again – particularly in the West and in NATO-aligned countries – highlighted the urgent need for underground shelters, bunkers, and other forms of protection from war and ongoing threats posed by the destruction of one or more of Ukraine's nuclear power plants, a threat made all the more understandable by recent dramatic representations of the Chernobyl nuclear disaster of 1986. The cold war bunker is not merely a thing of the past. Rather considering these nuclear and military threats, bunkers continue to be imagined in relation to Canadian COG measures (Brewster 2017). Additionally, prominent apocalyptic fears now mean that domestic bunker business in Canada and elsewhere is "booming" (Last 2022). And so, whether bunkers operate to manage anxieties or are remediated for purposes of interest, play or pleasure, it seems that, for now at least, we may never make it out of the bunker and that we may never return to a life unthreatened by precarity and collective media scarcity.

The entertainment bunker of today and its remediation of the cold war past tells us a great deal about media scarcity and its politics: the strategy of redundancy used to ward off the threat of scarcity served to ensure the continuity of a regime of abundance that necessitated longstanding disparities that continue today. In the event of nuclear war, Canadian identity might live on, but the average Canadian certainly would not, as they were superfluous to government survival. Moreover, COG planners arguably did nothing to address the survivability of those who lived outside of the mainstream abundant culture of Canadian society: the unhoused who had no chance of finding shelter, impoverished refugees struggling to plant roots, those locked behind bars and utterly forgotten, the Indigenous population on Indian reserves and their stolen children at Residential Schools, and so on. Redundancy represents a key problematic for a politics of media scarcity as it lays bare the contradictions and disparities embedded within an ideology of abundance. Bunker media's strategy of engineered redundancy was never designed to protect those groups and identities that truly understand what it means to live underground. Ironically, only those who knew the luxury of living openly would be the ones privileged to take cover if attacked. The pre-existing conditions of abundance and inequity ensure that those who have always had more are less likely to lose everything. This is perhaps the main message from the abundant and redundant underground that we hope will see the light of day.

Notes

1 The media redundancy of bunkers foreshadows their contemporary remediation as supposedly ultra-secure data centres (Taylor 2023). "Redundant equipment" (417) and protective architecture remains a defining feature of bunkers in their data centre form, articulating a logic of data preparedness that is meant to stave off "the unending prospect of data loss or IT system failure" (405), or what frame in terms of media scarcity.
2 Incidentally, this underground transmitter facility would become the subject of a later conspiracy about a second secret Diefenbunker in Carp (King 2014, 2015).
3 https://davescoldwarcanada.com/home/the-diefenbunker/the-iconorama-in-the-federal-warning-centre-cfs-carp-ceghq/.
4 A virtual tour of the Diefenbunker Cold War Museum can be found here: https://diefenbunker.ca/virtual-tours/.

Bibliography

Bennett, Luke. 2017. "Approaching the Bunker: Exploring the Cold War through Its Ruins." In *In the Ruins of the Cold War Bunker: Affect, Materiality and Meaning Making*, 3–22. Lanham: Rowman & Littlefield.

Bowers, Rachael, and Kevin Booth. 2017. "Preserving and Managing York Cold War Bunker: Authenticity, Curation and the Visitor Experience." In *In the Ruins of the Cold War Bunker: Affect, Materiality and Meaning Making*, edited by Luke Bennett, 201–214. Lanham: Rowman & Littlefield.

Boyer, Paul. 2005. *By the Bomb's Early Light: American Thought and Culture at the Dawn of the Atomic Age*. Chapel Hill: University of North Carolina Press.

Brewster, Murray. 2017. "Canada Sets Aside Two Bunkers at Military Bases amid Global Uncertainty, North Korean Threat | CBC News." *CBC*. November 29, 2017. https://www.cbc.ca/news/politics/north-korea-canada-cold-war-plan-1.4424523.

Burtch, Andrew. 2009. "If We Are Attacked, Let Us Be Prepared: Canada and the Failure of Civil Defence, 1945–1963." Doctor of Philosophy, Ottawa, ON: Carleton University. https://doi.org/10.22215/etd/2009-06530.

Burtch, Andrew. 2012. *Give Me Shelter: The Failure of Canada's Cold War Civil Defence*. Vancouver: UBC Press.

Campbell, Norman. 1961. "Carp War Shelter for Federal Government". *Ottawa Citizen* April 11.

Campbell, Rebecca. 2017. "Canada under the DEWline." *Journal of Canadian Studies* 51 (1): 112–133. https://doi.org/10.3138/jcs.51.1.112.

CBC Docs, dir. 2018. *What Secrets Lie Beneath North Bay, Canada? A Nuclear Bunker for One.|CBC Short Docs*. https://www.youtube.com/watch?v=z4QMb-_JtlY.

CBC News. 2021. "Diefenbunker Museum Gets $1.1M for 'Crucial Upgrades'=." *CBC*. January 22, 2021. https://www.cbc.ca/news/canada/ottawa/diefenbunker-museum-funding-upgrades-1.5841177.

Clearwater, John. 2006. *'Just Dummies': Cruise Missile Testing in Canada*. Calgary: University of Calgary Press.

Cocroft, Wayne, and Roger J. C. Thomas. 2003. *Cold War: Building for Nuclear Confrontation 1946–1989*. Ann Arbor: University of Michigan Press.

Colbourn, Susan. 2018. "'Cruising toward Nuclear Danger': Canadian Anti-Nuclear Activism, Pierre Trudeau's Peace Mission, and the Transatlantic Partnership." *Cold War History* 18 (1): 19–36. https://doi.org/10.1080/14682745.2017.1370456.

CTVNews, dir. 2015. *The Diefenbunker: Canada's Most Famous Bunker*. Carp, ON. https://ottawa.ctvnews.ca/the-diefenbunker-canada-s-most-famous-bunker-1.2466810.

Deachman, Bruce. 2022. "Diefenbunker to Get $600k Facelift." *Ottawa Citizen*. July 6, 2022. https://ottawacitizen.com/news/local-news/diefenbunker-to-get-600k-facelift.

Diefenbunker: Canada's Cold War Museum, dir. 2021. *2021 Artist-in-Residence Mairi Brascoupé: Making Akìmazinàzowin*. https://www.youtube.com/watch?v=e_ae3wJTpfQ.

Diefenbunker Museum. 2019. "The Bank of Canada Vault." Diefenbunker Museum. October 1, 2019. https://diefenbunker.ca/the-bank-of-canada-vault/.

Diefenbunker Museum. n.d.-a. "About the Diefenbunker." *Diefenbunker Museum*. n.d.-a. https://diefenbunker.ca/about-the-diefenbunker/.

Diefenbunker Museum. n.d.-b. "Artist-in-Residence." Diefenbunker Museum. n.d.-b. https://diefenbunker.ca/artist-in-residence/.
Diefenbunker Museum. n.d.-c. "Escape the Diefenbunker." n.d.-c. *Diefenbunker Museum.* n.d.-c. https://diefenbunker.ca/escape-room/.
Diefenbunker Museum. n.d.-d. "Rentals." n.d.-d. *Diefenbunker Museum.* n.d.-c. https://diefenbunker.ca/rentals/.
DMI (Diefenbunker Museum on Instagram). 2015. Instagram. November 1, 2015. https://www.instagram.com/p/9kCTeutu_G/.
DMI (Diefenbunker Museum on Instagram). 2017. Instagram. September 1, 2017. https://www.instagram.com/p/BYgPF0uBQ9e/.
DMI (Diefenbunker Museum on Instagram). 2018a. Instagram. February 8, 2018. https://www.instagram.com/p/Be8G8DzBSCh/.
DMI (Diefenbunker Museum on Instagram). 2018b. Instagram. September 19, 2018. https://www.instagram.com/p/Bn6039AHgA8/.
"Enter The Bunker – Historic Entertainment in Debert, Nova Scotia." n.d. Enter the Bunker. Accessed September 17, 2022. https://enterthebunker.xyz/.
Flintham, Matthew. 2020. "Vile Incubator: A Pathology of the Cold War Bunker." *Journal of War & Culture Studies* 13 (1): 11–32. https://doi.org/10.1080/17526272.2019.1687987.
GBS (Great Big Story). 2016. *The Nuclear Bunker Preserving Movie History.* https://www.youtube.com/watch?v=smXWZDupnkw.
Government of Canada. 1961. "Your Basement Fallout Shelter: Blueprint for Survival No. 1." Queen's Printer.
Government of Canada. n.d. *Let's Face It: Civil Defence Is Necessary.* Poster.
Graham, Stephen. 2016. *Vertical: The City from Satellites to Bunkers.* London: Verso.
Innis, Harold A. 1927. *The Fur Trade in Canada.* Toronto: University of Toronto Library.
Innis, Harold. 2008. *The Bias of Communication,* 2nd edition. Toronto; Buffalo, NY: University of Toronto Press.
Johannesson, Brian. 2011. "Carp Memories." https://secureservercdn.net/166.62.112.219/z94.3f0.myftpupload.com/wp-content/uploads/2020/03/carpmemories.pdf?time=1584060376.
Keane, John. 2013. *Democracy and Media Decadence.* Cambridge: Cambridge University Press.
King, Andrew. 2014. "Canada's Other Top-Secret Bunker." *Ottawa Citizen.* 2014. https://ottawacitizen.com/news/local-news/the-other-top-secret-bunker.
King, Andrew. 2015. "King: The Hunt for Our Other Diefenbunker." *Ottawa Citizen.* 2015. https://ottawacitizen.com/news/local-news/king-the-hunt-for-our-other-diefenbunker.
Kinnear, Sean L. 2020. "Reopening the Bunker: An Architectural Investigation of the Post-War Fate of Four Scottish Nuclear Bunkers." *Journal of War & Culture Studies* 13 (1): 75–96. https://doi.org/10.1080/17526272.2019.1688987.
Klinke, Ian. 2018. *Cryptic Concrete: A Subterranean Journey into Cold War Germany.* RGS-IBG Book Series. Hoboken, NJ: John Wiley & Sons Ltd.
Lajeunesse, Adam. 2007. "The Distant Early Warning Line and the Canadian Battle for Public Perception." Canadian Military Journal summer: 51–59.
Last, John. 2022. "Bunker Makers Say Business Is Booming — but There's a Reason Governments Left Bomb Shelters behind|CBC News." *CBC.* April 3, 2022. https://www.cbc.ca/news/world/bunker-business-1.6405487.
Ling-Temco Electronics. 1961. "NORAD." Worthpoint. 1961. https://www.worthpoint.com/worthopedia/1961-norad-colorado-ling-temco-137983960.

Maloney, Sean. 2012. "Dr. Strangelove Visits Canada: Project Rustice, Ease, and Bridge, 1958–1963." *Canadian Military History* 6 (1): 42–56.
Maloney, Sean M. 2020. *Deconstructing Dr. Strangelove: The Secret History of Nuclear War Films*. Lincoln: University of Nebraska Press.
Manning, Bill. 2003. "Beyond the Diefenbunker: Canada's Forgotten 'Little Bunkers.'" *Material Culture Review*, January. https://journals.lib.unb.ca/index.php/MCR/article/view/17956.
Masco, Joseph. 2009. "Life Underground: Building the Bunker Society." *Anthropology Now* 1 (2): 13–29.
Matthews, Sara, and Justin Anstett. 2015. *Finding Diefenbunker: Canadian Nationalism and Cold War Memory*. Waterloo: Wilfrid Laurier University Press.
McCamley, Nick. 2016. *Cold War Secret Nuclear Bunkers*. Illustrated edition. Barnsley, South Yorkshire: Pen and Sword.
McConnell, David. 1998. "Plan for Tomorrow ... TODAY!: The Story of Emergency Preparedness Canada, 1948–1998." Government of Canada Publications. D82-44/1998E-IN. https://publications.gc.ca/site/eng/90955/publication.html?wbdisable=true.
McEnaney, Laura. 2020. *Civil Defense Begins at Home: Militarization Meets Everyday Life in the Fifties*. Princeton: Princeton University Press.
McLuhan, Marshall. 1964. *Understanding Media: The Extensions of Man*. 2nd edition. Signet Book. New York: New American Library.
McLuhan, Marshall. 1969. "Distant Early Warning Playing Cards." The Marshall McLuhan DEW-Line Newsletter.
McLuhan, Marshall, and Bruce R. Powers. 1989. *The Global Village: Transformations in World Life and Media in the 21st Century*. Communication and Society. New York: Oxford University Press.
Ottawa Citizen, dir. 2018. *King: The Hunt for Our Other Diefenbunker*. https://www.youtube.com/watch?v=-jP4plHwB6M.
"Our Projects Through the Decades." n.d. Defence Construction Canada. Accessed September 16, 2022. https://www.dcc-cdc.gc.ca/about-dcc/our-history/our-projects-through-the-decades.
Ozorak, Paul. 2012. *Underground Structures of the Cold War: The World Below*. Barnsley: Pen & Sword Military.
Panneton, Daniel. 2015. "Diefenbunker, Canada's Cold War Museum." In *The Canadian Encyclopedia*. https://www.thecanadianencyclopedia.ca/en/article/diefenbunker.
Parikka, Jussi. 2012. *What Is Media Archaeology?* London: Polity.
Peters, Dave. n.d. "The ICONORAMA (in the FWC at CFS Carp / CEGHQ)." Dave's Cold War Canada. Accessed September 17, 2022. https://davescoldwarcanada.com/home/the-diefenbunker/the-iconorama-in-the-federal-warning-centre-cfs-carp-ceghq/.
Rafferty, Kevin, Jayne Loader, Pierce Rafferty, Archives Project, and Facets Video, dirs. 1982. *The Atomic Cafe*. New York: First Run Features.
Richemond-Barak, Daphné. 2018. *Underground Warfare*, 1st edition. New York: Oxford University Press.
Rose, Kenneth D. 2001. *One Nation Underground: The Fallout Shelter in American Culture*. American History and Culture. New York: University Press.
Schneider, Erin. 2010. "Apocalyptic Architecture: Cold War Bunkers, Reuse and the Everyday Landscape." Accessed March 11, 2022. https://www.academia.edu/440251/Apocalyptic_Architecture_Cold_War_Bunkers_Reuse_and_the_Everyday_Landscape.

Stokes, Paul. 2017. *Drakelow Unearthed Revised Edition: The Secret History of an Underground Complex*. Dudley: Black Country Press.

Strömberg, Per. 2013. "Funky Bunkers: The Post-Military Landscape as a Readymade Space and a Cultural Playground." In *Ordnance: War + Architecture & Space*. London: Routledge: 67–81.

Taylor, ARE. 2023. "Concrete Clouds: Bunkers, Data, Preparedness." *New Media & Society* 25 (2): 405–430. https://doi.org/10.1177/14614448221149936.

TBTV (TOP BOX TV), dir. 2021. *Canada's MASSIVE Cold War Bunker - Secrets Of The Exhibit 103 - Diefenbunker*. https://www.youtube.com/watch?v=L314I883Uu4.

The Ottawa Journal. 1961. "NORAD." May 16, 1961.

Toronto Telegram. 1961. "This Is The Diefenbunker!" September 11, 1961.

"UNC (Underground NORAD Complex)." 2021. *Underground NORAD Complex* (blog). July 19, 2021. https://noradcomplex.ca/2021/07/19/about-the-underground-norad-complex/.

USAADS (U.S. Army Air Defense School). 1965. "United States Army Air Defense Digest." U.S. Army Air Defense School. http://ed-thelen.org/USArmyAirDefense-Digest1965.html.

Vanderbilt, Tom. 2002. *Survival City: Adventures among the Ruins of Atomic America*, 1st edition. New York: Princeton Architectural Press.

Virilio, Paul. 1994a. *Bunker Archaeology*. Princeton: Princeton Architectural Press.

Virilio, Paul. 1994b. *The Vision Machine*. Bloomington, IN: Indiana University Press.

"VMWARA (Vintage Military, War and Army Recruiting Ads of the 1960s)." n.d. Accessed September 17, 2022. https://www.vintageadbrowser.com/military-ads-1960s.

Wilson, Louise K. 2020. "Sounds from the Bunker: Aural Culture and the Remainder of the Cold War." *Journal of War & Culture Studies* 13 (1): 33–53.

6 Conclusion
Future politics of media scarcity

In titling our book, *The Politics of Media Scarcity*, we have sought to explore the different forces, choices, priorities, and privileges involved when a community retreats or otherwise tries to hide their identity from the glare of media. Much of our attention has focused on the mediation of such media scarce individuals and communities or the lack thereof. But in this concluding chapter we begin by highlighting the specific *political* aspects of media scarce storytelling, as perhaps a means of reminding readers of the wider interventions articulated or more subtly implied within the book's pages. After this short introduction and justification in a way for the book's title, we turn our focus to the main concept of the book, scarcity in abundance, as articulated in each of the book's chapters and specific case studies. We then end this concluding chapter with a discussion of the future politics of media scarcity, specifically where it intersects with – and hopefully might contribute to – like-minded theories, projects, and political agendas.

While our book's introduction served to provide context to our central arguments and case studies, it also sought to highlight the political implications of scholarly knowledge. We began the book, in other words, by arguing that media abundance is not a natural or universal condition. Symbols and claims to economic abundance had long been made by ruling classes to legitimize their hold on political power. The same logic holds for *media* abundance. Not all contemporary societies, communities, or individuals are media abundant. Yet, at the same time, the world *has*, in general, become increasingly media abundant. The politics of media scarcity though is not merely posited as a "market" battle over scale or degrees, over how much media and information we should each have. It is not a third space or a fuzzy middle between plenty and scarcity. Rather we have argued that media scarcity is an underground form of communication, one that evades the glare of the abundant media landscape. Media scarcity derives in part from the need to be protected, secure, and sometimes anonymous. The politics of media scarcity serves to recognize the precariousness of being identified by media, and subsequently of communicating and understanding such experiences. In short, we claimed that holistic theories of media and communication could not simply ignore the political struggles that derived from media scarce conditions and histories.

Secondly, all our chapters emphasized the political context and history of media scarcity, the legacy of mediated relationships, particularly for certain marginalized communities. Social and political conflicts can force people underground as peoples' lives are threatened if left unprotected or unconcealed. This was evident with South African apartheid, incarceration in an era of fraught Indigenous reconciliation, and cold war conflict. Media scarcity is likely to be found in every space of political struggle and crisis. In the light of this, what is the consequence for marginalized communities when we are living in such politically troubled times, what some have dubbed the "permacrisis" (Turnbull 2022) – of ever stacking crises and conflicts? Media scarce communities are most likely only growing in number and precarity as millions are forced to hide, flee, or combat the impact of climate change, war, persecution, or genocide.

Our third definition of the politics of media scarcity is the most important, as it recognizes the media scarce themselves. It is a politics of resistance, of recognition, of history, and of identity. There is a political struggle over stories, over official narratives, and over the truth. For those communities that have gaps in their mediated past, their lives do not simply disappear. Nor do the media scarce lose their voice or place in the world. That said, the media abundant world is a demanding one, an unrelenting 24/7 one that certainly privileges the thoughts and opinions of the extrovert far more obviously than the covert. Abundant media power is increasingly a default setting, an embedded practice in everyday life. We should therefore hardly be surprised by claims that media platforms offer a pluralistic space of freedom, choice, and recognition, ironically terms that are deeply rooted in political debates, contests, and often armed conflicts.

Scarcity in abundance

In recognizing that media is abundant, but not universal, we conceptualized media scarce histories and communities as a scarcity in abundance, a relationship. Media scarcity is typically an expression of difference, injustice, alienation, or marginalization. Moreover, it is apparent how media scarce individuals and communities can be more easily identified in a social context that involves the valorization of abundance because such a condition more readily exposes any deviation from norms (or rather myths) of plenty. Simply put, people begin to stand out from a crowd when they fail to conform to expectations of media abundant participation. As a result, media scarce marginalization must be read as an issue that is nested within a culture and sociotechnical climate of abundance. For instance, as the practicalities of abundance become increasingly normalized as a requirement for social participation and

Conclusion: future politics of media scarcity 83

integration, it becomes increasingly difficult to lead an underground life for purposes of resistance, disobedience, or survival. To clarify, when the banal mediation of quotidian life – from daily selfies, food photography, and confessional posts – is a typical practice, those who do not make such regular posts or, worse, refuse to create online public accounts are commonly perceived as "ghosts" – individuals whose attempts to remain invisible are seen as cause for suspicion, distrust, or even fear by their peers or by governments and institutions. Who are they hiding from? What do the media scarce have to hide?

A different approach to the question of scarcity in abundance lies in investigating how power-knowledge asymmetries (re)produce relations of abundances or relative degrees of plentifulness. For instance, incarcerated people as well as their families, friends, and allies might experience a severely impoverished or deprived state of communication access. However, the ongoing integration of expansive technological systems of surveillance in carceral spaces shows that surveillance not only works to further curtail the communication freedoms of prisoners but also works to produce an abundance of information about these marginalized groups. This abundant, surveillant media apparatus – devices, datasets, and technologies – further challenges the ability of journalists, lawyers, activists, and researchers to communicate with – and advocate for – incarcerated individuals and populations.

Lastly, scarcity in abundance can also be understood through the metaphor of a needle in a haystack. Abundance can be weaponized or harnessed with bad intentions to deliberately cover a minor (yet incriminating) detail and what is otherwise small, obscure, quiet, or easily overlooked. This is a commonly practiced strategy for corporate litigators who may inundate the opposing party with unrelated or inconsequential documents during discovery to distract, confuse, exhaust, or otherwise outmanoeuvre their efforts to locate an important piece of evidence. Put simply, it becomes harder to find something small (in size or number) in the context of abundance. This scarcity in abundance furthermore highlights the challenge of knowing what to look for, of fully knowing the media scarce past and stories.

Even during the African National Congress' globally mediated battle against apartheid rule, the dynamics of scarcity in abundance were at play. In Chapter 2, we emphasized how the media scarce history and stories of uMkhonto we Sizwe (MK) continue to be overshadowed by the media rich and visually iconic history of the ANC and its iconic leader, Nelson Mandela. The predominant history and visual campaign of apartheid struggle in South Africa represents an enduring yet partial story. While MK were once protected by their media scarce tactics – avoiding the gaze of the apartheid state and police – today, their inability to draw upon media documents and records from the past challenges their appeals for contemporary recognition. MK histories, stories, and contributions to the end of apartheid are limited by a dual-sided form of media scarcity in which operatives were both unknown and unknowing – living according to a secret identity and never privy to a complete picture of the MK's operations. Many MK veterans never fully knew their roles or identities. These are stories that in many ways cannot be post mediated because the media scarce relationship of the MK was designed to leave gaps and fragmented accounts – so that, in the event of an operative's capture, less could be forcibly uncovered and known by the apartheid regime. Yet by being invisible to one another – and in many ways to themselves – MK continue to grapple with media scarcity.

Despite their lack of media documentation, MK engaged in an infrastructural form of media scarce resistance. Letter bombs were synchronized as spectacular performances to assure supporters of the presence and power of MK while tactically contributing to apartheid resistance by misdirecting the South African state and police. This covert infrastructure was dependent on the cover stories or "legends" of MK operatives lived and performed by individuals. The underground life of MK operatives, as with undercover life in general, was psychologically taxing and alienating, as a single slip-up could lead to personal targeting, and so, from this internalized precarity, even today many MK veterans refrain from telling stories about their media scarce past. This persistence of media scarcity into the present tells a story about the tactics and necessity of communication for those who are forced to live in the shadows.

By comparison, in Cheryl L'Hirondelle's *Why the Caged Bird Sings*, the challenge of scarcity in abundance comes to the fore through the concept of tracking, a media scarce tactic that lays pathways of resistance for others to follow and retell. Unlike the concept of the divide which figures prominently in discussions of media power in carceral institutions and elsewhere, tracks of resistance run along and push beyond infrastructural affordances – finding and imagining new possibilities of storytelling, ceremony, and community from within highly prohibitive and disciplined environments. In absolute contrast with the intensive and pervasive surveillance underpinning the array of media technologies that figure in carceral spaces, L'Hirondelle's co-written songs and recordings with incarcerated collaborators – primarily Indigenous women – refuse to reproduce such an extractive logic, but instead represent the voices, identities, and words within a multimedia infrastructure that extends to audiences far and wide. Representation online and in art galleries imparts an invitation for audience members to cross a divide – to take up and carry these songs. In the case of the installations for "Here I Am (Bless My Mouth)", this maintains an aesthetic of precarious scarcity expressed by grainy video quality and fragmented vocal performances, all re-staged by proxy visitor/allies. This beautiful yet incomplete songbird call reminds us of the gaps and absences inherent in media scarce communication while providing a commentary on the injustices of carceral power within colonial states such as Canada. Colonial institutions have continuously worked to silence the languages, songs, and oral customs of Indigenous people in Canada by forcibly separating them from their communities and stories. L'Hirondelle's tracking is committed to the creation and maintenance of ceremony, of coming together and regifting the music that lives within her in order to visit and sing with those who have been incarcerated.

L'Hirondelle's media scarce art and its many iterations involve endless searching and gathering as she continues to track down her collaborators on social media to record their voices and pay out the royalties they have earned. This is no easy task as many of her collaborators continue to lead unstable lives of media scarcity in abundance – offline or still locked away. Carceral media scarcity shapes and seriously limits the possibilities for storytelling and connection from conditions of incarceration. Seen from this view, media scarcity reminds us how carceral power can be maintained, reproduced, and amplified by systematically shaping how incarcerated populations can communicate and represent themselves. Tracks of resistance do not break down prison walls or overcome the precarity of media scarce life but remind us of the persistence that is needed to properly hear those who are systematically silenced. Media scarce art can move us in a direction of change when we are otherwise distanced and divided from the perspectives and stories that are needed to propel collective action. L'Hirondelle invites audiences to sit with these women so that together we might imagine and push forward with anti-colonial pathways of decarceration.

In Chapter 4, the overarching issues of scarcity in abundance take on yet different dynamics. In the case of Soviet secret cities, relative abundance was assured for those living in a media scarce but secure world. These communities were not forced into a life of media scarcity like other media scarce communities. Yet tragically, residents later learned about the radioactive toxicity of this relatively "protected" environment, articulating a precarity in abundance that was assured through media scarce regulations and control. Thus, secret cities allowed a good yet toxic life. Historically, the authoritarian life of secret cities was largely embraced by inhabitants due to the relative benefits and privileges that came with it. This speaks to a subjectification within media scarce communities that is largely lost when we imagine secret cities today as empty and stagnant in their politics. Rather, the media scarcity of closed cities forces us to inquire about and imagine the lives of media scarce communities that suffered from this governance strategy and biopolitical experiment. This imaginary project is at the heart of Sergey Novikov's artist collaboration, where former secret city residents reperform their former lives as media scarce subjects, re-presenting the human cost of political, environmental and economic toxins.

Novikov's media scarce art unlocks the storytelling potency of secret cities at a time when new economic experiments and tax-free zones have facilitated tax avoidance, public oversight, and government regulation. The media scarcity of secret cities and their unique economic privileges is analogous to other forms of media scarce hegemony today, such as wealth offshoring whereby the ultra-rich not only avoid taxation but avoid documentation of their wealth. In doing so, media scarcity can be used by the powerful as cover for socially toxic strategies that maintain and deepen social and economic inequalities. For the rich and powerful, the good yet toxic life might not seem so bad so long as one remains closed off from the human and environmental costs of such media scarce strategies.

Finally, in Chapter 5, we reflected on the generalized condition of precarity once represented by the terrifying threat of nuclear conflict, a media scarce condition that embraced a redundant form of protection for the future. The cold war created a political climate of abundant preparation, of digging in to hopefully withstand a nuclear blast and the following radioactive fallout. However, during this time, the bunker was not only a place of survival, but it became media straddling the line between concealment and communication. Bunker media functioned to deter its intended use, an underground infrastructure steeped in a logic of redundancy. It is through redundant bunker media that the threat of scarcity was both represented and prepared for, a grim reminder that the underground life could never compare with the comforts and privileges of the abundant life above.

Redundancy shows how myths of material and media abundancies paper over issues of scarcity/precarity in abundance. During the cold war, redundant Diefenbunker media served as the foundation for continuity of government planning in Canada, a project that would never protect the lives of ordinary subjects, especially of those who belonged to marginalized communities. Technologically sophisticated engineered redundancies ensured government resiliency and military power while rendering human redundancies – lives that would not be factored into the preparations for the future. The contemporary remediation of bunkers, as with the Diefenbunker Cold War Museum, invites a discussion of how redundancy mediates relations of scarcity/precarity in abundance in other spaces. For instance, in the music industry – with similarities in other creative industries – streaming platforms have created an ever tightening "digital enclosure" (Andrejevic 2007, 2022) of abundant media consumption that fails to fairly compensate artists and independent record labels. Meanwhile artificial intelligence (AI) music start-ups freely harvest this online cornucopia of musical creativity as training data for the generation of copycat content – a cycle of redundant production that disempowers artists within a culture of abundance. Perhaps we should look to the underground for answers to this exploitative configuration, the subcultural music scenes and communities that have always shied away from media abundant participation. Indeed, the underground has always seemed to question the merits of abundant life while striving to remake the politics of media scarcity into something more than a battleground for basic survival.

Future politics of media scarcity

In this book, we have focused extensively on media scarce art as a way to explore the politics of media scarcity. This has included discussion of photography, documentary film, song writing, and multimedia installations. In this area, we have only begun to scratch the surface. We are particularly intrigued by the prospect of combining auto-ethnographic methods with different forms of art practice as a way to counter media scarce relations. For instance, Marlon Fuentes's *Bontoc Euology* (1995) tells a compelling story as the film-maker searchers for answers about his ancestral roots by taking a great deal of creative license in reconstructing phonographic recordings collected of Indigenous Philippine informants by American ethnographers in the early 20th century. Oliva Landry (2022), building off Jeanette Hoorn (2002), argues that this mode of auto-ethnography refutes Spivak's argument that "the subaltern cannot speak" (2004) – that is, represent its own alterity as a colonized subject. Much like the media scarce, the subaltern is typically faced with "an injunction to silence" (102). Yet Landry's (2022) reading of *Bontoc Euology* shows how auto-ethnography can re-story and post-mediate "one's own history as a colonized subject not as a means of subjugation but as historiographical mode of self-expression that is both reflexive and unsettling" (126).

Another epistemological tradition that we did not discuss at any length in this book is based on a politics of refusal, on the rejection of dominant, abundant mythologies and hierarchies in an effort to create liberatory spaces and future. Take, for example, the Mohawk political anthropologist Audra Simpson who imbues media scarce politics in her Indigenous research design through the concept of "ethnographic refusal" "where she refuses to tell the whole story" (2014, 34). There are deliberate gaps and absences in her Haudenosaunee research as she "sought a way to respect and honor the individual privacy of people and the ethics of collective representation within deeply asymmetrical fields of power" (198). This choice of ethnographic refusal is designed to echo the sovereign politics of refusal practiced by the Haudenosaunee. Unlike the "recognition" that is so highly esteemed in multicultural politics, Mohawk refusal is a "political and ethical stance that stands in contrast to the desire to have one's distinctiveness as a culture, as a people, recognized…Those of us writing these issues can also 'refuse'"(11). Moreover, the argument of our book concerning scarcity in abundance is analogous to Simpson's concept of "nested" sovereignty (12). The Kanien'kehá:ka continue to resist against the ongoing colonization and settler logics of elimination in North America, and their refusal to be recognized for their difference clearly implicates a media scarce politics. Refusal denotes a wish to not be fully seen or heard but to instead embody a nested form of sovereignty. Although media scarce marginalization must be recalled as an issue that is nested within a culture of abundance, so too might media scarce empowerment.

88 Conclusion: future politics of media scarcity

Many Indigenous thinkers argue for modes of political refusal that articulate an anti-colonial politics of media scarcity. For instance, the Métis visual artist and scholar, David Garneau, proposes the concept of "irreconcilable spaces of Aboriginality" (2016, 26) to characterize the need for distance and non-Indigenous inaccessibility in times of reconciliation. Dylan Robinson (Stó:lō) whose writing appeared in Chapter 3 performs such a refusal in his book *Hungry Listening* (2020) by including nine pages of text that are intended to remain unread by non-Indigenous readers: "I ask that you stop reading by the end of this page. I hope you will rejoin us for Chapter 1" (25). This irreconcilable space of Aboriginality nested within a book to be read by all asks non-Indigenous readers to respect Indigenous peoples claims for a politics of media scarcity in abundance.

A politics of refusal has also been long mediatized by photography critics. For example, in *Potential History*, Ariella Aïsha Azoulay argues that photography is inherently violent as it was built on colonial logics and the "right to take" (2019, 280). Thus, she calls for a general strike of photographers to demand reconciliation and redress of imperial history. She writes:

> Imagine photographers refraining from going to "conflict zones," not fueling the endless thirsty corporations with more images that signal to them that the terrain is ready for further interventions…Imagine photographers not taking new photographs of imperial disaster…Imagine photojournalists and "concerned photographers"…going on strike and ceasing to fuel the voracious machine of news, archives, terror, shock, and fear.
>
> (281–282)

Azoulay calls for a disruption of the work that powers much of our media abundant structures. What would such a retreat into media scarcity help to unsettle about the assumptions and biases that underly predominant systems of media production, consumption, and circulation? Beyond this, what would a world of scarce images force us to politically acknowledge and reimagine?

Of course, the political efficacy of an organized strike stems from the power of collective action. Similarly, a media scarce politics will not move forward only with individuals but with media scarce communities. Yet how can allyship be practiced with such groups? Media abundant groups must commit to ways of supporting the media scarce – an abundance *beside* scarcity perhaps. This does not entail a politics of giving voice to the "voiceless", but rather might consist of at least two things: of respecting the desire/needs of scarcity of these communities while also speaking out against their ongoing oppression by strategies of surveillance and political silencing, which are likely to cause them to retreat further underground.

A future politics of media scarcity then might bear similarities with privacy claims, as a boundary control mechanism: a desired degree of privacy rarely involves a state of complete or permanent isolation or a void of communication. However, as a social boundary, relations of privacy function to protect forms of communication, such as sensitive topics, unpopular opinions, or unfamiliar ideas. Put simply, privacy can create and sustain underground spaces. Similarly, while coercive media scarcity is unbearable, a desired degree might be necessary to live a life that is inherently different from the norm – of a subculture, a minority, or a new community. Critiques of privacy often contend that it is too individualistic and too steeped in liberal commitments (Stalder 2002). However, in our view, privacy can also become media that is as "socially realized structures of communication" (Gitelman 2006, 7): more, specifically, privacy can be mediatized to communicate anti-oppressive politics while creating communicative space and breathing room for those in the underground. The legal scholar Scott Skinner-Thompson argues just this through the concept of "performative privacy" (2020), communicative acts that demonstrate an expressive opposition to an ever-expanding surveillance society and its logic of subordination: "When a person wears a hoodie or mask shielding their identity, they may be engaged in a form of active, expressive resistance to the surveillance regime – lodging an objection to being surveilled" (45). Privacy *communicates*, and similarly, we are interested in the stories, identities, and messages that take shape in and through conditions of media scarcity.

Skinner-Thompson maintains that protection of performative privacy is particularly important for marginalized communities, such as racialized minorities and queer communities, because of their disproportionate targeting in societies. In our framework, performative privacy might become a tactic of media scarce resistance – one of abundance beside scarcity – whereby those outside of marginalized communities voluntarily take up underground, secretive behaviours as a form of allyship with the media scarce. As an example of this, we would like to draw on Chris Gilliard and his anti-surveillance intervention around photography and media recording. In a hybrid online seminar at the University of Michigan, Digital Studies Institute, Gilliard objected to any media recording and refused to turn his camera on over Zoom. This refusal to participate in media abundant norms was deeply generative, creating space for critical ideas to be openly discussed. Incessant documentation can confine and suppress – a media abundant chilling effect. However, as a Black theorist of race and technology, why should Gilliard be the only one in a room of participants to take up such a responsibility to problematize the conditions of constant recording and sharing in our abundant media/surveillance culture? What if those outside of marginalized communities similarly refused to have their photos taken and be recorded? What would this communicate? How could this media scarce position create more space for those in the underground?

Whatever the tactic, media scarce stories, moments, pauses, or silences can at the very least counter the myth of endless media riches, adding lived experiences to our understanding of media power. So long as this scarcity in abundance remains at the margins, and its politics unrecognised, this will perpetuate issues of precarity, inequality, and discrimination that are obscured within a culture of abundance. The more media becomes infused in our everyday lives and cultures, the more glaring and jolting the media scarce intervention becomes. From this, we hope that a politics of media scarcity can be reclaimed to disrupt the mediatized routine, demands, and belief in the invisible hand of abundant media power.

Bibliography

Andrejevic, Mark. 2007. "Surveillance in the Digital Enclosure." *The Communication Review* 10 (4): 295–317. https://doi.org/10.1080/10714420701715365.

Andrejevic, Mark. 2022. "Meta-Surveillance in the Digital Enclosure." *Surveillance & Society* 20 (4): 390–396. https://doi.org/10.24908/ss.v20i4.16008.

Azoulay, Ariella Aïsha. 2019. *Potential History: Unlearning Imperialism*. London; Brooklyn, NY: Verso.

Fuentes, Marlon, Bridget Yearian, Cinema Guild, and National Asian American Telecommunications Association, dirs. 1995. *Bontoc Eulogy*. New York: Cinema Guild.

Gitelman, Lisa. 2006. *Always Already New: Media, History, and the Data of Culture*. Cambridge, MA: MIT Press.

Hoorn, Jeanette. 2002. "Captivity, Melancholia and Diaspora in Marlon Fuentes' Bontoc Eulogy: Revisiting Meet Me in St Louis." In *Body Trade*. London: Routledge. 195–207.

Landry, Olivia. 2022. *A Decolonizing Ear: Documentary Film Disrupts the Archive*. Toronto: University of Toronto Press.

Robinson, Dylan. 2020. *Hungry Listening: Resonant Theory for Indigenous Sound Studies*. Minneapolis: University of Minnesota Press.

Robinson, Dylan, Keavy Martin, and David Garneau. 2016. "Imaginary Spaces of Conciliation and Reconciliation: Art, Curation, and Healing." In *Arts of Engagement*, 21–42. Ed. D. Robinson & K. Martin. Waterloo: Wilfrid Laurier University Press.

Simpson, Audra. 2014. *Mohawk Interruptus: Political Life Across the Borders of Settler States*. Illustrated edition. Durham: Duke University Press.

Skinner-Thompson, Scott. 2020. *Privacy at the Margins*. Cambridge; New York: Cambridge University Press.

Spivak, Gayatri Chakravorty. 2004. "Can the Subaltern Speak?" In *Imperialism*. Ed. Peter Cain & Mark Harrison. London: Routledge. 171–219.

Stalder, Felix. 2002. "Privacy Is Not the Antidote to Surveillance." *Surveillance & Society* 1 (1): 120–124. https://doi.org/10.24908/ss.v1i1.3397.

Turnbull, Neil. 2022. "Permacrisis: What It Mean and Why It's the Word of 2022." *The Conversation*. Accessed October 20, 2023. https://theconversation.com/permacrisis-what-it-means-and-why-its-word-of-the-year-for-2022-194306.

Index

Note: *Italic* page numbers refer to figures and page numbers followed by "n" denote endnotes.

abundance: assumption of 61; celebration of 4; challenge of scarcity 84; culture of 4, 82; definition of 4; dynamics of scarcity 83; economic abundance 73, 81; images of sustenance 4; media scarce resistance 89; post-cold war bunker 62; scarcity/precarity in 86; social participation 82–83; sociotechnical climate 82; *see also* media abundance
Abundance: On the Experience of Living in a World of Information Plenty (Boczkowski) 2
abundant preparation 61; political climate of 86; underground existence 64
African National Congress (ANC) 10, 14
Andrejevic, Mark 3
anti-apartheid media campaign 17
anti-apartheid struggle 10, 16
anticolonial principles 11
anti-communist ideology 68
apartheid-era police 10
apocalyptic media scarcity 12
armed propaganda campaign 18, 25
artificial intelligence (AI) 3, 62, 86
atomic bomb 1, 66
The Atomic Café 68
atomic cities 44
attention economy 5
auto-ethnographic methods 87
Azoulay, Ariella Aïsha 88

Beck, John 63
Benjamin, Ruha 9

Bennett, Luke 64
Bishop, Sarah 17
Black emancipation 9
Black slavery and racism 9
"Blueprint for Survival" 68
Boczkowski, Pablo 2–3
Bontoc Euology (Fuentes) 87
Boyer, Paul 68
Brascoupé, Mairi 74
Browne, Simone 8, 53
Brown, Kate 44, 45, 51
Bunker Archaeology (Virilio) 63
bunker media/bunkerology 12, 61, 72, 73–74; cultural power 63; definition of 63; genesis of 63–65; geology of 63; military conflicts 63; redundancy of 65; remediated 71–72; into urban fabric 64; *see also* underground

Campbell, Maria 41n1
Canada: Cold War Museum 71; domestic bunker business in 76; as front line of the apocalypse 65–66; Indigenous people in 85
Canadian Broadcasting Corporation (CBC) radio 71
Canadian bunker media 62–65, 68
Canadian Forces Station Carp 69
carceral infrastructure 31
carceral media scarcity 32, 36
carceral reform, anti-colonial track 32
CEGHQ (Central Emergency Government Headquarters) 69
ceremonial infrastructure 11, 32, 38, 40, 41

Index

ceremonial society 33, 35, 41
Chak, Tings 20
Chernobyl nuclear disaster 75
Cherry, Janet 14–15
climate catastrophe 66
climate changes 2
Closed Cities (Sailer) 46, 48, 50
cold war: bunker media 61, 63, 75; existential threat of 61
Cold War Museum 12, 62, 71, 72
colonialism 5, 8, 21, 31, 33
communications 4, 11, 17, 18, 19, 20, 29, 70, 81; holistic theories of 82; network 32; practices 2
Communist Party of South Africa 15
concentration camp 20
contemporary political campaigns 17
continuity of government (COG) planners 64
COVID pandemic 74
Cuban missile crisis 61
cultural abundance 1
cultural agenda 68

Dark Matters: On the Surveillance of Blackness (Browne) 8
Dawn: Journal of Umkhonto we Sizwe 20–21, 26n3
decarceration 10, 30, 32, 85
decolonial struggles 16
Diefenbaker, John 62, 66, 73
Diefenbunker Cold War Museum 86
Diefenbunker media 70–71; internal verticalization of 70
digital: documents 5; enclosure 86; infrastructure 2
Distant Early Warning system 65
documentary film 6, 21
documents: conceptualization of 7; digital documents 5; online documentation 34; political documents 7; social media objects 17; socio-technical documents 7; transformative pathway 35; underground lives 5

Easterling, Keller 44
East German Stasi 72
economic abundance 81
economic security 45
environmental scarcity 29
environmental threats 2

ethnographic refusal concept 87
expert tracker 31
Extrastatecraft: The Power of Infrastructure Space (Easterling) 44

Facebook 2, 34
fallout-proof bunkers 68
Federal Civil Defence Coordinator 69
Flintham, Matthew 63
Fogarty-Valenzuela, Benjamin 20
forced migration 2, 17
Foucault, Michel 57
Fuentes, Marlon 87

Garneau, David 88
Gilliard, Chris 89
Gitelman, Lisa 7
Google 2, 44
Goto, Ayumi 37
Graham, Stephen 70
Gready, Paul 22–23
guerrilla movement 10

Hani, Chris 22
Hegeler, Edward C. 4
"Here I Am (Bless My Mouth)" 35, 36, *39*, 84
home bunker 68
Hoorn, Jeanette 87
The Hope Factory (Meshchaninova) 55–56
human redundancy 62
Hungry Listening (Robinson) 31, 88
hydrogen bombs 66

iconic secret cities 53–57
ICONORAMA system 70–71
"Indigenous ontologies of song" 35
Indigenous people 31, 33
Indigenous reconciliation 74
Infoglut: How too Much Information Is Changing the Way We Think and Know (Andrejevic) 3
Instagram 7
institutional surveillance 38
International Brigade Against Apartheid (Kasrils) 22
internet revolution 2
Ionia: Land of Wise Men and Fair Women (Craig) 1
"irreconcilable spaces of Aboriginality" 88

Jenkin, Tim 22

Karppinen, Kari 3
Kaspar-Eisert, Verena 46
Kasrils, Ronnie 22, 24
Kaun, Anne 29
Keable, Ken 19, 20
King Ferdinand VII 3
Kinnear, Sean L. 63
kinship 9, 41n1
Klinke, Ian 63, 64, 72
Korean War 66

Landry, Olivia 87
The Language of New Media (Manovich) 6
legends 16, 17, 20, 23–25, 84
L'Hirondelle, Cheryl 11, 30, 31, 34, 41n1, 84, 85
life stories 21–24
listening, Western mode of 35
Lomasko, Victoria 20
Lomax, Alan Jr. 35
London Recruits (Keable) 22
Looking Backward, 2000–1887 (Bellamy) 1

"Maggie Paul's round dance song" 32
Mahlangu, Solomon 21
Mandela, Nelson 10, 14, 15, 21
Margaret Sewap case 35–36
material scarcity 3
McLuhan, Marshall 65
media: digitization of 6; discriminatory power of 3; documentation 16, 44, 84; holistic theories of 82; individual's role 14; infrastructure 2, 6, 17; landscape 3, 17; objects 6, 7; wireless infrastructure 2
media abundance 3, 6, 81; conceptual turn 2; consumer culture 68; contemporary culture of 30; culture of 29; definition of 2, 5; environment 6; ideologies of 3; *see also* abundance
media power 3, 12, 62, 82, 84, 90
media scarcity 4, 5–7, 6, 9, 18, 25, 38, 60, 61, 72; anti-colonial politics 88; authoritarian life of 45; cold war politics of 74; communication 18, 25; communities 60; disciplinary policies of 31; flexibility of 23; imaginary of 29; kinship and inspiration 9; media strategies 19–21; military objects 18; political context 62, 66, 81, 82, 87; protective form 17; secret cities 54; storytelling 16, 25, 57; vital importance 30
medical surveillance 53
Meshchaninova, Natalia 55
methodology of visiting 31
military surface infrastructure 63
Miner, Dylan 31
Miyohtakwan Music 34
Motseothata, Kebotlhale 26n4
multi-mediated propaganda war 19

NATO-aligned countries 75
Norilskino project 56–57
Novikov, Sergey 11, 46, 50, 53, 55, 85
nuclear missile testing 65
nuclear war 61, 72

Okimaw Ohci Healing Lodge 36, 38
O'Neill, Kevin Lewis 20
online documentation 34

Pantieras, Christos 74
Parikka, Jussi 61
perestroika (economic reform) 48
performative privacy 89
personal media objects 7
photograph *47, 48, 54*; art-photograph projects 11, 46; *Closed Cities* collection 46; critics 88; fiction 57; projects 46; rural Saskatchewan 40; Soviet secret cities 44
Plutopia (Brown) 45, 51, 53
post-apartheid visual campaign 14
post-cold war bunker 62
post-Soviet secret cities 49
Potential History (Azoulay) 88
power-knowledge asymmetries 83
precarity 8
prison media 11; concept 29; framework of 29; infrastructure of 33
prison visitation 32; plexi-glass partition 38
Putin, Vladimir 53, 75

redundancy, definition of 63
religion, Japanese symbols of 4
Richardson, Bill 48
Richemond-Barak, Daphné 64
Robinson, Dylan 31, 35

Sailer, Gregor 11, 46, *47, 48,* 50
scarcity in abundance 5, 8, 16, 20, 62, 82–85, 87, 90
Schneider, Erin 72
Schreiber, Rebecca 17
Second World War 63
secret cities 44, 46; citizen subjects of 52; "class-less" society 45; environmental hazards of life 53; media documentation 57; storytelling potency of 85; ZATO photographs 51
self-produced media 2
Skinner-Thompson, Scott 89
smartphone 2; camera app 7
social media 2, 17, 32, 34, 60
sonorous bridge 37
sousveillance 8
South Africa: apartheid rule in 26n1; British Colonialism in 21; security police 14
South African Police 23
Soviet closed cities 56
Soviet Gulag 55
Soviet secret cities 44, 85
Soviet Union 44, 54
Spear of the Nation (Cherry) 15
Spivak, Gayatri Chakravorty 87
Spreadable Media 6
Stiernstedt, Fredrik 29
"The Strong Woman Song" 32–33
surveillance 8, 9, 29, 35–38, 52, 64, 70, 83, 88–89

Tarde, Gabriel 1, 2, 61
tax credits 48–49
tax-free zones 49
Thatcher, Margaret 49
thermonuclear war 66, 75
TikTok 7
tracking 30, 31, 34, 35, 38, 40
Truth and Reconciliation Commission 21

uMkhonto we Sizwe (MK) 10; anti-apartheid media campaign 17; bomb campaigns 19; *Dawn: Journal of Umkhonto we Sizwe* 20; decolonial struggles 16; formation of 15; informal networks 19; Military Veterans Association 14; post-1979 campaign 19; relative scarcity 16; storytelling 20; testimonials 21–24
underground: as front line of the apocalypse 66–69; as lifestyle choice 60; politics 65; *see also* bunker media/bunkerology
Underground Man (Tarde) 1, 9
Underground Railroad 9
The Undocumented Everyday: Migrant Lives: and the Politics of Visibility (Schreiber) 17
Undocumented Storytellers: Narrating the Immigrant Rights Movement (Bishop) 17
Undocumented: The Architecture of Migrant Detention (Chak) 20
United States' Strategic Air Command 70
"Unseen Places" (Sailer) 46
urban cold war bunkers 64
US Atomic Energy Commission 66
US-Canada missile tracking system 70

Vanderbilt, Tom 63
vertical axis of surveillance 64
Virilio, Paul 63
visiting: anti-colonial practices of 31; L'Hirondelle's practice of 33
Vogt, Tristan 21
Voices from the Underground (Gunn and Haricharan) 22

Wells, H.G. 1
Why the Caged Bird Sings (L'Hirondelle) 11, 30, 32, 34, 84

Zakrytye Administrativno-Territorial'nye Obrazovaniya (ZATO) 46, 48, 52, 53; Archipelago 58n2; *Norilskino* stages 56–57; secret city project 55
Zuckriegel, Margit 47

For Product Safety Concerns and Information please contact our EU representative GPSR@taylorandfrancis.com
Taylor & Francis Verlag GmbH, Kaufingerstraße 24, 80331 München, Germany

www.ingramcontent.com/pod-product-compliance
Lightning Source LLC
Chambersburg PA
CBHW050843160426
43192CB00011B/2131